Artificial Intelligence in Operations: Strategy, Efficiency, and the Future of Execution

Published 2026 by River Publishers
River Publishers
Broagervej 10, 9260 Gistrup, Denmark
www.riverpublishers.com

Distributed exclusively by Routledge
605 Third Avenue, New York, NY 10017, USA
4 Park Square, Milton Park, Abingdon, Oxon OX14 4RN

Artificial Intelligence in Operations: Strategy, Efficiency, and the Future of Execution / Ahmed Banafa.

Routledge is an imprint of the Taylor & Francis Group, an informa business

ISBN 978-87-438-1291-3 (paperback)
ISBN 978-87-438-1294-4 (online)
ISBN 978-8-743-81293-7 (ebook master)
ISBN 978-87-438-1296-8 (ePub)
DOI: 10.1201/9788743812937

Artificial Intelligence in Operations: Strategy, Efficiency, and the Future of Execution

Ahmed Banafa
San Jose State University, USA

River Publishers

Routledge
Taylor & Francis Group
NEW YORK AND LONDON

Dedication

This is book is dedicated to my amazing son Abdulhamid and his family

Contents

Preface

Operations have always been the engine of organizational performance. What has changed is the intelligence embedded within that engine.

This book *Artificial Intelligence in Operations: Strategy, Efficiency, and the Future of Execution* was written in response to a growing gap between AI hype and operational reality. While many discussions focus on algorithms or futuristic visions, far fewer address how AI actually transforms day-to-day execution—how goods move, decisions are made, services are delivered, and institutions function under pressure.

Across business, government, healthcare, education, and defense, AI is shifting operations from reactive to predictive, from manual coordination to autonomous systems, and from static planning to continuous adaptation. These changes demand new skills, new governance models, and new ethical frameworks.

The chapters in this book are designed for practitioners, students, and decision-makers who need clarity rather than buzzwords. Each domain-specific section explores not only what AI enables, but also what can go wrong when systems are poorly designed, poorly governed, or blindly trusted.

Ultimately, this book argues that operational excellence in the AI era is not defined by automation alone, but by *responsible integration*—aligning technology, people, data, and strategy. AI will shape the future of execution, but leadership will determine whether that future is resilient or fragile.

Target audience (who will read this book)

This book is primarily written for:

- **Operations and supply chain leaders.** Managers and directors responsible for optimizing business processes, logistics, manufacturing, and service operations using AI-driven tools.
- **Business executives and strategic decision-makers.** CEOs, COOs, CIOs, and senior leaders seeking to leverage AI for operational efficiency, resilience, and competitive advantage.
- **Graduate students and faculty (MBA/MS programs).** Students and instructors in operations management, business analytics, supply chain, and AI-in-business courses.
- **AI and digital transformation professionals.** AI product managers, data scientists, automation specialists, and enterprise technology leaders implementing AI in real-world operations.
- **Public sector, healthcare and education administrators.** Leaders managing large operational systems in government, healthcare, higher education, and public services.

List of Abbreviations

AI	Artificial intelligence
ML	Machine learning
NLP	Natural language processing
RPA	Robotic process automation
IoT	Internet of Things
AGV	Automated guided vehicle
UAV	Unmanned aerial vehicle
AWS	Autonomous weapons systems
UGV	Unmanned ground vehicle
WMS	Warehouse management system
SCM	Supply chain management
VR	Virtual reality
AR	Augmented reality
LAWS	Lethal autonomous weapon systems
HR	Human resources

About the Author

Prof. Ahmed Banafa is a globally recognized expert in the fields of artificial intelligence (AI), blockchain, cybersecurity, and the Internet of Things (IoT). With a distinguished career that spans research, operations, and strategic technology management, he has been a prominent voice in shaping the discourse around emerging technologies.

He has received numerous accolades for his work, including the Certificate of Honor from the City and County of San Francisco, the Haskell Award for Distinguished Teaching from the University of Massachusetts Lowell, and the prestigious Author & Artist Award from San Jose State University. In 2018, LinkedIn named him the No. 1 Tech Voice to Follow, highlighting his foresight and influence in technology trends.

Prof. Banafa's thought leadership has been featured in Time, Nature, Forbes, IEEE Spectrum, and the MIT Technology Review. He has been a guest expert on global media outlets such as ABC, CBS, NBC, FOX, Bloomberg, BBC, NPR, Reuters, and NHK, providing insights on cutting-edge technology topics. He is also a contributing member of the MIT Technology Review Global Panel, further cementing his role as a respected thought leader.

An accomplished author, Prof. Banafa has written several acclaimed books, including:

- *Secure and Smart Internet of Things (IoT) Using Blockchain and Artificial Intelligence (AI)*—Winner of the SJSU Author and Artist Award and ranked among the best technology books of all time.

- *Blockchain Technology and Applications*—Adopted into curricula at prestigious universities, including Stanford.
- *Quantum Computing*—Officially added to the Library of Congress collection.
- *Transformative AI* and *Introduction to AI* (2025)—Both received the SJSU Author and Artist Award.
- His upcoming work, *AI in Action*, marks his ninth book and explores AI's real-world impact across industries.

Prof. Banafa studied cybersecurity at Harvard University and digital transformation at the Massachusetts Institute of Technology (MIT). He holds a master's degree in electrical engineering and a Ph.D. in artificial intelligence.

Introduction

Operations are where strategy becomes reality. For decades, organizations competed on efficiency, scale, and cost optimization. Today, that foundation is being fundamentally reshaped by artificial intelligence (AI). No longer confined to analytics dashboards or automation scripts, AI is now embedded directly into the core of operational decision-making.

This book *Artificial Intelligence in Operations: Strategy, Efficiency, and the Future of Execution* examines how AI is transforming operations across industries and institutions. From supply chains and logistics to healthcare systems, national security, higher education, criminal justice, diplomacy, and modern warfare, AI is redefining how work is planned, executed, monitored, and optimized.

Unlike purely technical texts, this book focuses on *operational impact*. It explores how AI enables predictive planning, adaptive execution, and autonomous coordination while also introducing new risks related to bias, governance, cybersecurity, workforce displacement, and accountability. Real-world case studies—from Amazon, Walmart, UPS, Tesla, and IBM to military, diplomatic, and public-sector systems—demonstrate how AI moves from theory to practice.

AI in operations is not about replacing humans. It is about redesigning workflows, redefining roles, and creating human–machine collaboration at scale. Organizations that understand this shift will gain resilience, agility, and strategic advantage. Those that do not risk inefficiency, fragility, and irrelevance.

This book provides a structured lens for understanding how AI reshapes operational systems—and how leaders can adopt it responsibly, strategically, and effectively.

CHAPTER

1

Artificial Intelligence in Operations: Transforming Business Efficiency and Strategy

Operations management has always been the heartbeat of business performance—linking strategy, resources, and processes to deliver value. In the last decade, artificial intelligence (AI) has moved from being a futuristic concept to an indispensable operational tool.

DOI: 10.1201/9788743812937-1

AI in operations extends beyond automation. It encompasses predictive analytics, process optimization, adaptive decision-making, and the creation of entirely new business models. From supply chains and manufacturing floors to HR departments and customer service desks, AI is altering the fundamentals of how organizations plan, execute, and adapt.

Foundations of AI in Operations

What AI Brings to Operations

AI contributes four primary capabilities to operational management:

- **Automation of routine tasks:** Replacing repetitive, labor-intensive work with intelligent systems.
- **Prediction and forecasting:** Using machine learning models to anticipate demand, risks, and customer behaviors.
- **Optimization:** Recommending efficient allocation of resources, schedules, and workflows.
- **Augmented decision-making:** Providing insights and simulations that help managers choose the best course of action.

These capabilities help companies achieve lower costs, higher speed, better quality, and greater adaptability.

Future managers and executives will not only supervise human teams but also oversee human–machine collaborations. This requires a new literacy: understanding algorithms, interpreting analytics, and framing ethical guidelines for responsible AI adoption.

AI in Supply Chain Operations

Demand Forecasting

AI models analyze historical sales, market conditions, social media trends, and macroeconomic signals to predict demand. Unlike traditional forecasting methods, these models continuously learn and adjust.

- **Example:** Walmart uses AI-driven demand forecasting to optimize inventory across thousands of stores. By analyzing weather patterns and local events, the system predicts spikes in demand for specific products (e.g., umbrellas before storms).

Inventory Optimization

Holding excess inventory ties up capital, while stockouts damage customer trust. AI tools balance these trade-offs by suggesting optimal reorder points.

> - **Example:** Amazon applies predictive analytics to manage millions of SKUs in its warehouses, ensuring rapid delivery without overstocking.

Logistics and Transportation

AI enhances route planning, fleet management, and real-time delivery tracking. Algorithms factor in traffic, fuel efficiency, and vehicle capacity.

> - **Example:** UPS's ORION system uses AI to reconfigure driver routes dynamically, saving millions of gallons of fuel annually and cutting carbon emissions.

AI in Manufacturing Operations

Predictive Maintenance

Sensors connected to AI systems monitor equipment performance. Instead of scheduled maintenance, repairs occur when the system predicts imminent failure.

> - **Example:** General Electric (GE) applies AI in its "Digital Twin" approach—creating virtual replicas of machines to forecast wear and tear, preventing costly downtime.

Quality Control

Computer vision systems inspect products at a microscopic level, detecting defects more accurately and faster than human inspectors.

> - **Example:** BMW employs AI cameras on assembly lines to detect imperfections in paint jobs, ensuring premium quality standards.

Smart Manufacturing

AI coordinates robotics, supply systems, and workforce scheduling into an adaptive "Industry 4.0" model.

- **Example:** Siemens integrates AI with IoT sensors to create self-adjusting manufacturing systems that reduce waste and improve efficiency.

AI in Service Operations

Customer Service

AI chatbots and virtual assistants provide 24/7 responses, reducing costs and improving customer satisfaction.

- **Example:** Bank of America's Erica virtual assistant manages millions of client interactions, handling balance inquiries, bill reminders, and financial advice.

HR and Workforce Management

AI tools streamline recruitment by scanning resumes, conducting initial candidate assessments, and predicting employee turnover.

- **Example:** Unilever uses AI-driven gamified assessments and video interview analysis to recruit talent worldwide, reducing hiring time by 75%.

Healthcare Operations

AI optimizes hospital bed allocation, appointment scheduling, and patient flow management.

- **Example:** Johns Hopkins Hospital uses AI to forecast emergency department volumes and assign staff dynamically.

AI in Financial and Risk Operations

Fraud Detection

AI systems analyze transaction patterns in real time to flag anomalies.

- **Example:** Mastercard uses AI-powered systems to block fraudulent transactions within milliseconds, saving billions annually.

Process Automation (RPA + AI)

Robotic process automation (RPA) enhanced with AI manages back-office tasks such as invoice processing, claims handling, and compliance checks.

- **Example:** Deloitte integrates AI-based RPA in finance departments, reducing manual workloads by up to 40%.

Strategic Implications for Operations Managers

Cost Efficiency vs. Innovation

AI delivers immediate cost reductions but also enables innovation—such as customized production, personalized services, and new revenue streams. Managers must balance efficiency with strategic differentiation.

Human–Machine Collaboration

Rather than replacing humans, AI often complements them. Managers must design workflows where employees focus on creativity, relationship management, and strategic thinking while AI handles repetitive tasks.

Ethics and Governance

AI introduces risks of bias, privacy violations, and overreliance on algorithms

Case Studies

Amazon's AI-driven Operations

- **Supply Chain:** Predictive demand modeling ensures fast delivery.
- **Warehouses:** AI-powered robots (Kiva) optimize item picking and packing.
- **Customer Service:** AI recommends products, boosting sales and loyalty.

Tesla's Smart Manufacturing

Tesla applies AI across design, production, and vehicle performance updates. Its factories use predictive analytics for machine maintenance, while vehicles continuously upload performance data to improve future models.

Zara's Fast Fashion Supply Chain

Zara leverages AI to track customer preferences and social media trends, rapidly adjusting production and distribution. This agility shortens design-to-shelf cycles, maintaining its competitive edge.

IBM Watson in Healthcare

Watson supports oncologists by analyzing millions of medical papers and patient data to recommend treatment options, improving operational efficiency in healthcare decision-making.

Future Directions

Autonomous Operations

Entire supply chains may run with minimal human intervention—self-driving trucks, AI-managed ports, and automated warehouses.

AI + Sustainability

AI is being used to minimize waste, improve energy efficiency, and track carbon footprints. Operations managers will increasingly measure performance not only in terms of cost but also environmental impact.

AI Factories of the Future

Concepts like "dark factories" (fully automated with no human workers) are emerging. While controversial, they highlight the efficiency potential of AI.

Generative AI in Operations

Generative AI will move beyond content creation into operations: generating optimized process designs, simulating supply chain scenarios, and even designing new business strategies.

Challenges in Implementation

- **Data quality:** AI systems are only as strong as the data they consume.
- **Integration costs:** High initial investment can deter small businesses.
- **Workforce resistance:** Fear of job displacement often causes pushback.
- **Cybersecurity risks:** AI systems can themselves become targets of attack.
- **Regulation uncertainty:** Governments are still drafting laws on AI use in operations.

Artificial intelligence is no longer optional in operations—it is essential. It enables businesses to become faster, leaner, and more adaptive while opening doors to innovation

Whether managing global supply chains, directing financial services, or running healthcare institutions, tomorrow's leaders must see AI as both a tool for efficiency and a compass for strategic growth. Those who learn to harness AI responsibly will not only optimize operations but also create competitive advantages that redefine industries.

CHAPTER 2

Artificial Intelligence in Logistics and Supply Chain: Transforming the Future of Global Operations

The logistics and supply chain sector is the backbone of global commerce. From sourcing raw materials to delivering finished products to consumers,

DOI: 10.1201/9788743812937-2

it orchestrates an intricate dance of suppliers, manufacturers, distributors, and retailers. Yet, supply chains are becoming increasingly complex due to globalization, rising customer expectations, geopolitical uncertainties, and disruptive events like pandemics and climate-related disasters.

Artificial intelligence (AI) is emerging as a game-changer in this environment. AI-powered systems provide companies with unprecedented abilities to predict demand, optimize routes, automate warehouses, manage risks, and personalize customer experiences.

The Evolution of Supply Chain Management

From Traditional Models to Digital Supply Chains

Historically, supply chain management (SCM) focused on efficiency: reducing costs, standardizing processes, and maximizing economies of scale. The linear flow—from suppliers to manufacturers to distributors to customers—dominated.

However, with the rise of e-commerce, globalization, and just-in-time manufacturing, supply chains became more dynamic and vulnerable to disruptions. Today's *digital supply chains* are characterized by real-time data, global interdependencies, and the need for agility.

The Role of AI in this Evolution

AI shifts supply chains from *reactive* to *predictive* and *prescriptive* systems:

- **Reactive:** Responding to problems after they occur.
- **Predictive:** Forecasting potential issues before they arise.
- **Prescriptive:** Recommending or autonomously executing optimal actions.

Key AI Technologies in Supply Chains

AI encompasses a spectrum of technologies, each with unique supply chain applications.

Machine Learning (ML)

- Identifies patterns in vast datasets (sales history, weather, social media trends).
- Enables demand forecasting, anomaly detection, and dynamic pricing.

Natural Language Processing (NLP)

- Automates customer service via chatbots.
- Extracts insights from unstructured data (emails, shipping documents, news feeds).

Computer Vision

- Monitors warehouse operations.
- Inspects product quality on assembly lines.
- Tracks cargo movement with smart cameras.

Robotics and Automation

- Autonomous guided vehicles (AGVs) in warehouses.
- Robotic arms for picking and packing.
- Drone deliveries.

Optimization Algorithms

- Route optimization for last-mile delivery.
- Inventory placement in regional warehouses.

Generative AI

- Creates supply chain scenarios for strategic planning.
- Automates document generation (contracts, invoices).
- Provides real-time simulations of global disruptions.

Applications of AI Across the Supply Chain

Demand Forecasting

Accurate demand forecasting prevents stockouts and overstocking. Traditional methods relied on historical sales, but AI incorporates:

- Market trends
- Seasonality
- Social media sentiment
- Economic indicators

- Weather data.

Example: Walmart uses AI to forecast demand spikes before hurricanes by analyzing past consumer behavior, predicting surges in items like bottled water and flashlights.

Inventory Management

AI-powered systems adjust inventory levels dynamically:

- **Predictive analytics** ensures safety stock without excess.
- **Computer vision** monitors shelves in real time.
- **IoT sensors** alert managers about perishable goods nearing expiration.

Example: Amazon's "anticipatory shipping" uses AI to pre-position products in warehouses near customers even before orders are placed.

Procurement and Supplier Management

AI evaluates suppliers on:

- Reliability
- Cost performance
- Sustainability
- Risk exposure.

Benefit: Companies can quickly switch suppliers in case of disruptions.

Example: IBM's Watson analyzes supplier risk using external data (geopolitics, financial health, natural disasters).

Transportation and Route Optimization

AI minimizes delivery times and fuel costs by analyzing:

- Traffic patterns
- Weather forecasts
- Fuel prices
- Vehicle availability.

Example: UPS's ORION (On-Road Integrated Optimization and Navigation) AI system reportedly saves 10 million gallons of fuel annually by optimizing driver routes.

Warehouse Automation

- **Robotic picking systems** increase speed and reduce errors.
- **AI-powered WMS (Warehouse Management Systems)** allocate space efficiently.
- **Computer vision** ensures safety and accuracy in operations.

Example: Ocado, a UK-based online grocer, operates highly automated warehouses with robots powered by AI coordination algorithms.

Last-mile Delivery

The most expensive and complex segment of logistics, last-mile delivery benefits from AI:

- Route optimization for couriers.
- Autonomous delivery robots and drones.
- Customer preference analysis for delivery windows.

Example: FedEx's SameDay Bot leverages AI to navigate sidewalks and deliver packages directly to homes.

Risk Management and Resilience

AI scans global news, weather reports, and trade data to predict:

- Port closures
- Political unrest
- Natural disasters.

This enables contingency planning and proactive risk mitigation.

Customer Experience

AI enhances customer satisfaction:

- Real-time tracking and delivery updates.

- Personalized recommendations.
- Chatbots for instant resolution of queries.

Benefits of AI in Logistics and Supply Chain

(1) **Cost reduction:** Lower fuel usage, efficient inventory management, and fewer errors.
(2) **Agility:** Quick adaptation to disruptions or demand changes.
(3) **Sustainability:** Optimized routes reduce carbon emissions.
(4) **Customer satisfaction:** Faster deliveries, personalized experiences.
(5) **Transparency:** End-to-end visibility builds trust with stakeholders.

Challenges and Risks

Despite its benefits, AI adoption faces hurdles:

- **Data quality & integration:** Supply chain data is often siloed and inconsistent.
- **High initial costs:** Robotics and AI infrastructure require significant investment.
- **Workforce displacement:** Automation reduces certain jobs, raising ethical concerns.
- **Cybersecurity risks:** Increased reliance on connected systems makes supply chains targets for attacks.
- **Algorithmic bias:** Poorly trained AI models may misinterpret signals, causing disruptions.
- **Regulatory and ethical issues:** Privacy, sustainability, and compliance must be balanced with efficiency.

Case Studies

Amazon

- Anticipatory shipping with predictive analytics.
- AI-powered warehouse robots.
- Customer personalization with recommendation engines.

DHL

- "Resilience360" platform monitors global risks using AI.
- Autonomous drones for inventory counting.

Maersk

- AI predicts shipping delays and optimizes routes across oceans.
- Blockchain integration for secure documentation.

Alibaba

- "Cainiao Smart Logistics Network" processes millions of orders daily with AI-driven efficiency.

The Future of AI in Logistics and Supply Chain

Autonomous Supply Chains

In the future, AI will drive fully autonomous supply chains where:

- Machines predict and place orders automatically.
- Autonomous vehicles deliver goods without human intervention.
- Smart contracts execute payments instantly.

Human–AI Collaboration

Rather than replacing humans entirely, AI will augment supply chain managers by:

- Handling repetitive tasks.
- Providing decision support.
- Freeing humans for strategic roles.

Integration with Emerging Technologies

- **Blockchain:** For transparent transactions.
- **IoT:** For real-time data collection.
- **Quantum computing:** For solving ultra-complex optimization problems.

Sustainability Focus

AI will play a vital role in *green logistics*, helping companies achieve net-zero carbon goals by optimizing energy use and reducing waste.

AI is not merely a tool for improving logistics—it is redefining the entire supply chain ecosystem. Companies adopting AI see enhanced efficiency, agility, and sustainability, while those lagging risk obsolescence. The supply chain of the future will be predictive, autonomous, and customer-centric, powered by AI at every step.

CHAPTER

3

Algorithms of War: The Rise of Generative AI on the Battlefield

In the ever-evolving landscape of warfare, technological advancement has always played a decisive role—from iron weapons to nuclear arms. But the 21st century has ushered in a more silent, intelligent, and invisible force reshaping the battlefield: algorithms. Among them, generative artificial intelligence (GenAI) is emerging not just as a tool but as a strategic actor, crafting decisions, creating tactics, and redefining the meaning of power projection.

DOI: 10.1201/9788743812937-3

The Algorithmic Turn in Warfare

Algorithms are step-by-step sets of rules designed to perform specific tasks. When integrated with massive datasets and high computing power, they evolve from simple calculators into decision-making engines. In warfare, this evolution marks a shift from human-led command structures to data-driven operations.

From Linear Command to Distributed Autonomy

Traditional warfare relied on hierarchical decision-making: a top-down approach where generals issued orders and soldiers executed them. Algorithmic warfare introduces a decentralized model where decisions can be made dynamically on the edge—by machines themselves. This model allows for faster reactions, adaptive planning, and real-time optimization.

The Data-driven Battlefield

Modern warfare generates an enormous volume of data—from satellite images and drone footage to social media feeds and battlefield sensors. Algorithms are essential to parsing, analyzing, and acting upon this information at speeds far beyond human capacity. The more data they digest, the more precise and predictive they become.

Why Does Generative AI Matter in War?

Generative AI refers to AI systems that can create new content—text, images, simulations, or code—based on patterns learned from large datasets. Unlike traditional AI, which classifies or predicts, GenAI *generates*. This capability has profound implications in the context of war.

Key Attributes of GenAI in Military Use, Figure 3.1

- **Autonomous creativity:** The ability to generate scenarios, war games, or adversarial simulations.
- **Language mastery:** Real-time translation, information warfare scripts, or policy briefings.
- **Tactical visualization:** Generation of synthetic battlefield environments for training or strategy development.
- **Code generation:** Automated writing or modification of software used in defense systems.

Figure 3.1 Key attributes of GenAI in military use.

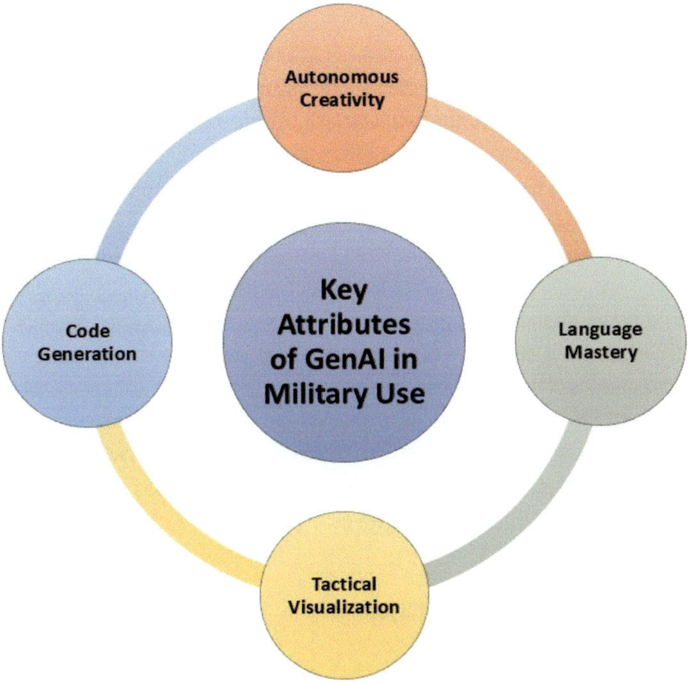

Strategic Applications of GenAI in Modern Warfare

(1) **Generating battlefield simulations.** One of the most valuable uses of GenAI is in creating immersive, realistic battle scenarios. Military strategists can test new tactics or simulate enemy maneuvers without deploying a single soldier. These simulations, enriched by generative models, can include variable terrains, weather, civilian populations, and even unpredictable enemy behavior.

Generative AI can also adjust the complexity of simulations based on evolving battlefield intelligence, ensuring that decision-makers and autonomous systems are training on the most relevant threats.

(2) **Accelerated weapon design and testing.** Traditionally, the development of new weapons could take years. GenAI shortens that timeline dramatically. By generating blueprints, structural simulations, and even material compositions, GenAI helps engineers prototype weapons systems digitally before a physical model is built.

Furthermore, generative design can suggest unconventional configurations that might elude human engineers—drone swarms with self-adaptive formations, for example, or underwater vessels optimized for stealth through biomimicry.

(3) **Cyber warfare and AI-generated malware.** In the cyber domain, GenAI can write malicious code or adapt existing code in response to evolving defenses. Adversarial GenAI can be used to develop polymorphic malware—malicious software that constantly changes its signature to evade detection.

It can also help generate social engineering scripts or deepfake content used to manipulate targets, plant misinformation, or destabilize communication channels within a military network.

(4) **Psychological and information warfare.** GenAI is a powerful tool for information operations. It can generate fake news, realistic deepfake videos, or synthetic personas at scale. These outputs can be tailored to specific audiences to exploit social divisions, shape public opinion, or sow confusion during conflict.

For example, a generative model could produce thousands of localized posts that subtly influence populations, soldiers, or leaders through algorithmically optimized narratives.

(5) **Autonomous decision support.** Generative AI also assists in battlefield decision-making. Given a set of parameters—enemy position, troop readiness, terrain constraints—it can generate a series of tactical options, predict outcomes, and even simulate consequences several moves ahead.

In high-pressure environments, commanders can use GenAI-generated battle plans as suggestions or starting points. These models continuously update as new data streams in, creating a living decision tree that evolves during battle.

The Emergence of AI-enabled Combat Systems

While GenAI doesn't directly fire weapons, it plays a critical role in enhancing the autonomy and precision of modern combat systems.

(1) **AI-generated swarm behaviors.** Drones or unmanned ground vehicles often operate in swarms. GenAI can be used to generate swarm behaviors—patterns of movement, coordination, and decision-making—that adapt to threats in real time. These algorithms give the swarm collective intelligence, allowing them to navigate obstacles, avoid attacks, or strike targets autonomously.

(2) **Adaptive camouflage and deception.** By analyzing sensor data, radar signatures, and environmental inputs, GenAI can generate camouflage patterns or electronic signals that confuse enemy systems. It can also simulate fake unit deployments or ghost armies on radar using decoy generation algorithms.

Training the Warrior of Tomorrow with GenAI

Human soldiers and officers are also benefiting from generative AI. Military education and training have been transformed through AI-generated simulations, gamified environments, and scenario planning tools.

(1) **Language and cultural training.** Generative models can create realistic role-playing exercises that involve foreign languages and cultural nuances. Trainees interact with AI-generated characters that mimic real-world behavior, preparing them for field operations in unfamiliar regions.

(2) **Emotional and ethical simulations.** Modern conflicts are not just physical—they are psychological and moral. Generative AI enables the creation of ethically complex simulations where soldiers must make life-and-death decisions involving civilians, allies, or moral dilemmas. These immersive environments help develop not only tactical skills but also moral reasoning.

Figure 3.2 Risks, challenges, and ethical frontiers.

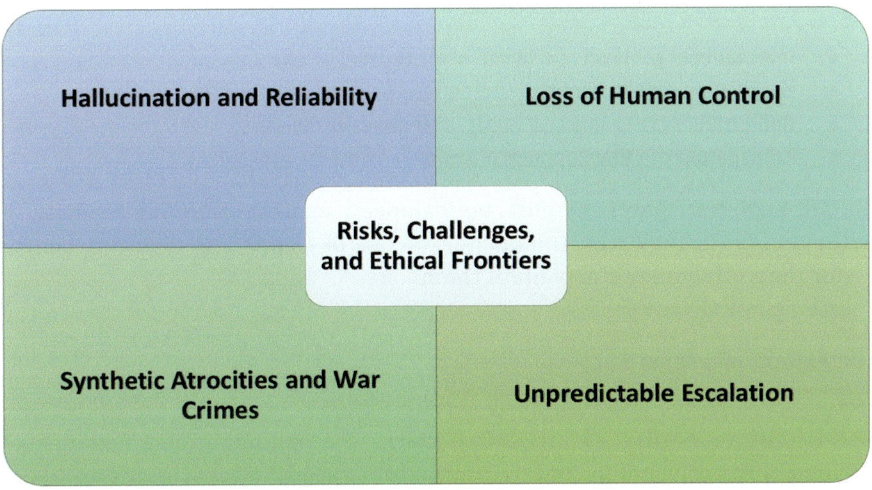

Risks, Challenges, and Ethical Frontiers, Figure 3.2

(1) **Hallucination and reliability.** One of the core risks with GenAI is the phenomenon known as "hallucination"—where the system generates plausible but incorrect information. On a battlefield, such an error could misinform commanders, cause friendly fire, or escalate conflicts.

(2) **Loss of human control.** As more decisions are outsourced to machines, the question arises: how much control should remain with human operators? If autonomous weapons systems act based on GenAI-generated inputs, the line between human intention and machine execution blurs dangerously.

(3) **Synthetic atrocities and war crimes.** There's also concern that GenAI could be used to fabricate war crimes—deepfakes showing atrocities that never occurred. Such content could

provoke retaliation, damage reputations, or derail peace negotiations. Verification mechanisms are struggling to keep pace with the sophistication of GenAI outputs.

(4) **Unpredictable escalation.** Generative models often operate in probabilistic ways, making their behavior hard to predict under new conditions. In the fog of war, GenAI might generate an unforeseen outcome—an aggressive maneuver, a flawed negotiation strategy, or a provocative action—without clear accountability.

Guardrails and Governance: The Next Battle

The governance of GenAI in warfare is still in its infancy. Existing treaties do not adequately cover the scope of algorithmic warfare or AI-generated operations. There is a pressing need for:

- **International protocols** on the ethical use of GenAI in combat.
- **Verification mechanisms** to detect and counter deepfakes or synthetic propaganda.
- **Audit trails** that ensure accountability for AI-generated decisions.
- **Transparency in development** of AI models for defense applications.

Military transparency must be balanced against national security, but without clear frameworks, the unchecked use of GenAI risks igniting conflicts faster than diplomacy can contain them.

The Algorithmic Arms Race

The rise of generative AI in warfare marks the beginning of a new era—not defined by firepower alone but by information, speed, and synthetic intelligence. Algorithms of war are not future concepts—they are present realities, embedded in the software of drones, the logic of missile guidance systems, the code of information campaigns, and the simulated worlds of defense strategists.

What distinguishes this era is the shift from destructive capability to *cognitive superiority*. Winning a war may no longer hinge on who has the most troops or tanks, but on who has the smartest algorithms—and who can use GenAI to outthink, outmaneuver, and out-create their adversaries.

As humanity steps into this new frontier, the challenge is not just technological—it is deeply philosophical. Can we build machines of war without becoming enslaved by them? Can we encode ethics into algorithms? And can we wage intelligent wars without losing our moral compass?

These questions will define not only the future of warfare, but the future of civilization itself.

CHAPTER

4

Autonomous Warfare: How AI and Drones Are Replacing Human Soldiers on the Battlefield

The nature of warfare is undergoing a radical transformation. In the past, wars were defined by boots on the ground, tanks in the field, and human decision-makers orchestrating strategies. However, the dawn of artificial intelligence (AI) has begun to reshape every facet of combat. From autonomous drones to AI-driven cyberattacks, the wars of tomorrow may not require human soldiers at all. This fusion of machine intelligence and military strategy has brought unprecedented capabilities—and profound ethical, technical, and geopolitical challenges.

DOI: 10.1201/9788743812937-4

The Evolution of Warfare: From Traditional to Technological

For centuries, the conduct of war relied on human physicality, intuition, and decision-making. From the hand-to-hand combat of ancient armies to the industrial-scale battles of the 20th century, human involvement was central. Even with the advent of missiles, aircraft, and submarines, it was humans who guided and controlled these tools.

However, the digital age ushered in a new era. The Gulf War in 1991, often called the first "network-centric war," showcased the role of satellites, surveillance, and precision-guided munitions. Since then, AI technologies have made inroads into intelligence analysis, battlefield logistics, and target recognition. But we are now crossing a critical threshold: AI is moving from a supportive role to an operational one, where it not only assists but acts autonomously.

Autonomous Weapons and AI-powered Drones: Shaping the Future of Combat

One of the most controversial developments is the emergence of lethal autonomous weapon systems (LAWS). These are weapons that can identify, select, and engage targets without direct human intervention. Examples include AI-enabled drones, robotic tanks, and sea-based autonomous vessels.

Drones, in particular, have revolutionized warfare. Once controlled remotely by human pilots, modern drones now integrate AI capabilities that allow them to navigate complex environments, identify targets, and execute missions with minimal or no human oversight. Swarm drones—groups of small, networked UAVs operating cooperatively—are especially potent. These systems can overwhelm defenses, confuse radar, and conduct coordinated strikes.

Autonomous drones and weapons systems provide several tactical advantages:

- **Extended reach:** AI-powered drones can operate in hostile territory without risking human lives.
- **Speed and precision:** Algorithms can process sensor data in real time, allowing for rapid decision-making.
- **Adaptability:** Machine learning allows drones to improve performance over time and adapt to changing mission environments.

The impact of these systems on warfare is profound. In modern conflicts, they have shifted the power dynamics, allowing even smaller nations or non-state actors to challenge larger powers. They enable surgical strikes, round-the-clock surveillance, and psychological pressure, while minimizing the exposure of human troops.

Critics argue that such autonomy removes human judgment from the kill chain, increasing the risk of unintended casualties and ethical violations. Proponents argue that AI systems can make more precise decisions under stress and reduce friendly fire and collateral damage. The question remains: should machines have the authority to take human lives?

Cyber Warfare: Invisible Battles in Digital Domains

While physical autonomous weapons dominate headlines, cyber warfare is arguably the most active front for AI deployment. Cyber operations can disrupt economies, disable infrastructure, steal secrets, and manipulate information at scale.

AI enhances cyber-attacks by enabling:

- **Automated vulnerability scanning:** AI tools can identify weak points in a system faster than human hackers.
- **Adaptive malware:** Malicious code that evolves based on environment or user behavior, evading detection.
- **Deepfake deception:** AI-generated content used to mislead or manipulate public opinion.
- **Phishing optimization:** AI can craft more convincing phishing emails by mimicking communication styles.

Conversely, AI also strengthens cyber defense. Intrusion detection systems now use machine learning to spot anomalies and anticipate attacks. Predictive analytics can identify threat patterns before they manifest. Still, as attackers and defenders both leverage AI, the stakes continue to rise.

Advantages of AI-driven Warfare, Figure 4.1

(1) **Speed:** AI systems can make decisions in milliseconds, far outpacing human reflexes.
(2) **Persistence:** Machines do not suffer fatigue, hunger, or emotional breakdowns.
(3) **Data integration:** AI can process terabytes of satellite, sensor, and signal data to provide situational awareness.
(4) **Risk reduction:** Removing soldiers from the battlefield reduces human casualties.
(5) **Force multiplication:** AI-powered drones and autonomous weapons allow a single operator to control multiple platforms.

Figure 4.1 Advantages, Risks and Challenges of AI-Driven Warfare

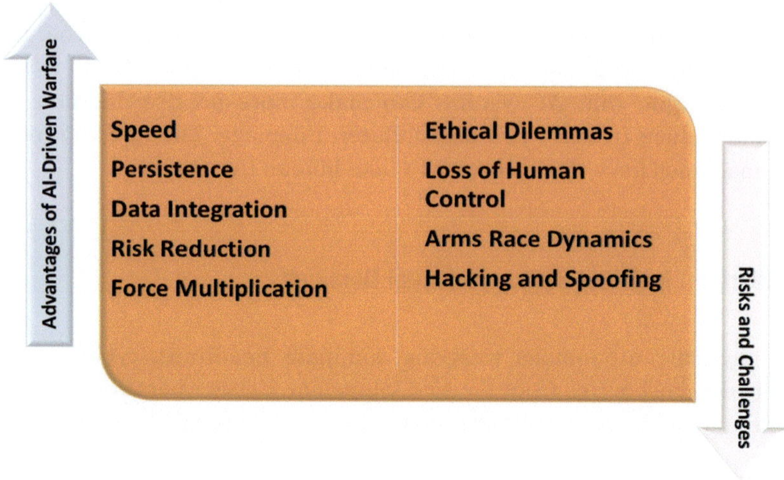

Risks and Challenges, Figure 4.1

(1) **Ethical dilemmas.** Who is responsible when an AI system makes a fatal mistake? Traditional accountability does not apply neatly to machines. The absence of moral reasoning in AI raises questions about proportionality, discrimination, and humane treatment in war.

(2) **Loss of human control.** As AI systems grow more complex, there is a risk of losing control. Emergent behavior in neural networks, unexpected decision pathways, and AI's black-box nature make it difficult to predict outcomes.

(3) **Arms race dynamics.** Nations are racing to develop superior AI military capabilities. This may reduce the threshold for conflict, as countries with advanced AI may feel emboldened to act without fear of reprisal. Moreover, proliferation to rogue states or non-state actors is a growing concern.

(4) **Hacking and spoofing.** AI systems can be compromised. Adversaries could spoof sensor inputs, manipulate training data, or inject adversarial noise, leading to catastrophic decisions by autonomous weapons.

International Response and Regulation

Calls for regulation of AI in warfare are growing. The United Nations has debated bans on autonomous weapons, and several NGOs, including the Campaign to Stop Killer Robots, advocate for legal frameworks.

However, major powers remain divided. The U.S., China, and Russia oppose a binding ban, preferring voluntary guidelines. Critics argue that this leaves the door open for misuse and escalation.

Some proposed principles include:

- **Human-in-the-loop:** AI can assist, but a human must approve lethal actions.
- **Transparency:** AI systems must be explainable and auditable.
- **Non-proliferation:** Restrictions on the sale or export of autonomous weapons to unstable regions.

The Role of Big Tech and Academia

Companies like Google, Microsoft, and Palantir are involved in military AI contracts, sparking internal debates about ethical use. Project Maven, a Pentagon AI initiative for video analysis, caused employee protests at Google.

Academic institutions are also central to AI development. Universities must balance research freedom with responsibility, ensuring that AI innovations are not easily weaponized.

The Human Factor: Soldiers, Strategists, and Civilians

Even in a future dominated by AI, humans are not obsolete. Soldiers will require new training in robotics, cybersecurity, and data interpretation. Strategists must understand AI's capabilities and limitations to craft effective doctrines.

Moreover, civilians are increasingly at risk in AI-driven conflicts. Cyber-attacks on critical infrastructure—power grids, hospitals, financial systems—can disrupt societies far from the battlefield. AI can amplify the reach of war without geographic boundaries.

Scenarios for the Future

(1) **AI deterrence and stability.** Just as nuclear weapons created a doctrine of mutually assured destruction, AI systems might deter aggression through superior capabilities. Automated defense networks could neutralize attacks before they begin.

(2) **Unintended escalation.** Autonomous systems reacting to ambiguous data could initiate conflicts. A false positive in missile detection or border intrusion could trigger retaliation without human oversight.

(3) **Hybrid warfare.** AI will likely be integrated into hybrid warfare strategies, combining cyber-attacks, propaganda, economic disruption, and kinetic action. The line between war and peace may blur.

(4) **AI arms control regimes.** International agreements, similar to nuclear treaties, may eventually govern AI use. Verification mechanisms, transparency mandates, and red lines will be essential to prevent abuse.

Navigating the Age of Machine Wars

AI is transforming the battlefield in ways once confined to science fiction. While it offers the potential to reduce human casualties and increase precision, it also introduces grave risks of miscalculation, loss of control, and ethical lapses.

The rise of AI-powered drones and autonomous weapons is fundamentally altering how wars are fought. These tools give militaries new reach and resilience but also introduce unprecedented dangers. Warfare is becoming faster, less human, and more complex.

Humanity must confront these challenges with foresight, cooperation, and regulation. The goal should not be to halt technological progress but to ensure it serves peace, not peril. As we enter this new era of warfare without human soldiers, the responsibility to guide AI's military use wisely rests with us all—engineers, policymakers, soldiers, and citizens alike.

The machine wars are no longer on the horizon. They have already begun. The question is whether we can master them before they master us.

CHAPTER

5

Artificial Intelligence (AI) in Modern Military Applications

Artificial intelligence (AI) is rapidly transforming numerous sectors of society, and the military domain is no exception. As armed forces worldwide seek to maintain technological superiority, AI has emerged as a critical area

DOI: 10.1201/9788743812937-5

of investment and development. This chapter explores the multifaceted applications of AI across different military branches, examines specific weapons systems enhanced by AI, and analyzes the advantages, disadvantages, and challenges associated with military AI. Additionally, we will look at future trends and discuss strategies to mitigate risks and preserve global security in an era of AI-powered warfare.

AI Applications Across Military Branches

(1) **Army:** The army is leveraging AI to enhance battlefield awareness, logistics, and combat effectiveness. Some key applications include:

- (a) Autonomous ground vehicles: AI-powered unmanned ground vehicles (UGVs) can perform reconnaissance, transport supplies, and even engage in combat operations with minimal human intervention.
- (b) Predictive maintenance: Machine learning algorithms analyze sensor data from vehicles and equipment to predict maintenance needs, reducing downtime and improving operational readiness.
- (c) Soldier performance optimization: AI systems monitor soldiers' physiological data to optimize training regimens and enhance combat performance.

(2) **Navy:** Naval forces are incorporating AI to improve maritime operations, undersea warfare, and fleet management:

- (a) **Autonomous ships and submarines:** AI enables unmanned surface and underwater vessels to conduct patrols, gather intelligence, and potentially engage in combat.
- (b) **Anti-submarine warfare:** AI algorithms process sonar data to detect and track enemy submarines more effectively than human operators.
- (c) Fleet management and logistics: AI optimizes naval logistics, predicting maintenance needs and managing supply chains for fleets at sea.

(3) **Air force:** AI is revolutionizing air combat, surveillance, and aerospace operations:

- (a) Autonomous drones: AI-controlled unmanned aerial vehicles (UAVs) can perform reconnaissance, engage targets, and even operate in swarms.
- (b) Pilot assistance systems: AI copilots assist human pilots in complex missions and potentially take over in emergency situations.
- (c) **Air traffic control**: AI systems help manage increasingly crowded airspace, both for military and civilian applications.

(4) **Space force:** As space becomes an increasingly important military domain, AI is playing a crucial role:

- (a) **Satellite management:** AI algorithms optimize satellite orbits, manage constellations, and predict potential collisions with space debris.
- (b) Space situational awareness: Machine learning enhances the tracking and identification of objects in orbit, improving space domain awareness.

(c) Autonomous space vehicles: AI-powered spacecraft could potentially conduct maintenance, refueling, or even offensive operations in space.

(5) **Cyber command:** In the realm of cyber warfare, AI is becoming an indispensable tool:

(a) Network defense: AI systems detect and respond to cyber threats in real-time, protecting military networks from attacks.

(b) Offensive cyber operations: AI can be used to identify vulnerabilities in enemy systems and automate cyber-attacks.

(c) Information warfare: Machine learning algorithms analyze and generate content for psychological operations and influence campaigns.

AI-enhanced Weapons Systems

(1) **Autonomous weapons systems (AWS):** Also known as "killer robots," these are weapons that can select and engage targets without meaningful human control. Examples include:

(2) **Missile defense systems:** AI enhances the speed and accuracy of intercepting incoming missiles:

(3) **Electronic warfare systems:** AI improves jamming, spoofing, and electronic protection capabilities:

(4) **Predictive maintenance systems:** AI optimizes equipment readiness and reduces maintenance costs:

Figure 5.1 Advantages and disadvantages of military AI.

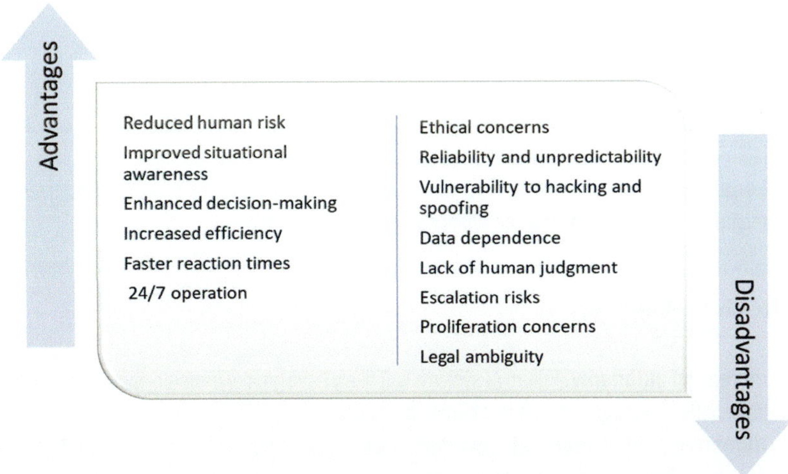

Advantages of Military AI, Figure 5.1

(1) **Enhanced decision-making:** AI can process vast amounts of data and provide rapid, data-driven recommendations to commanders.
(2) **Improved situational awareness:** AI-powered sensors and analysis tools provide a more comprehensive and accurate picture of the battlefield.
(3) **Reduced human risk:** Autonomous systems can perform dangerous tasks, potentially saving soldiers' lives.
(4) **Increased efficiency:** AI optimizes logistics, maintenance, and resource allocation, reducing costs and improving operational effectiveness.
(5) **Faster reaction times:** AI-enhanced systems can respond to threats more quickly than human operators, potentially providing a critical advantage in combat.
(6) **24/7 operation:** Unlike human operators, AI systems can function continuously without fatigue, maintaining constant vigilance.

Disadvantages of Military AI, Figure 5.1

(1) **Ethical concerns:** The use of autonomous weapons raises significant moral questions about the role of human decision-making in warfare.
(2) **Reliability and unpredictability:** AI systems may behave unpredictably in complex, real-world scenarios, potentially leading to unintended consequences.
(3) **Vulnerability to hacking and spoofing:** AI-powered systems could be compromised by adversaries, potentially turning weapons against their operators.
(4) **Data dependence:** AI systems require vast amounts of high-quality data to function effectively, which may not always be available in combat situations.
(5) **Lack of human judgment:** AI may struggle with nuanced decision-making that requires empathy, cultural understanding, or complex ethical considerations.
(6) **Escalation risks:** The speed and efficiency of AI-powered warfare could lead to rapid escalation of conflicts, potentially increasing the risk of large-scale war.
(7) **Proliferation concerns:** As AI technology becomes more accessible, there is a risk of it falling into the hands of non-state actors or rogue nations.
(8) **Legal ambiguity:** The use of autonomous weapons systems raises complex legal questions regarding accountability and compliance with international law.

Future Trends in Military AI

(1) **Increased autonomy:** Future AI systems will likely have greater decision-making capabilities, potentially operating with minimal human oversight.
(2) **Human–machine teaming:** Advanced AI will work alongside human soldiers, enhancing their capabilities and decision-making processes.

(3) **Swarm intelligence:** Large groups of autonomous drones or robots will coordinate their actions to achieve complex objectives.

(4) **Quantum AI:** The integration of quantum computing with AI could lead to unprecedented processing power and problem-solving capabilities.

(5) **AI-powered hypersonic weapons:** AI may enable the development of more accurate and maneuverable hypersonic missiles.

(6) **Cognitive electronic warfare:** AI will enhance electronic warfare capabilities, enabling systems to adapt to and counter enemy tactics in real-time.

(7) **Predictive analytics for geopolitical events:** AI could be used to forecast potential conflicts and inform strategic decision-making.

Strategies for Maintaining Global Security

(1) **International regulations and treaties:** Developing comprehensive international agreements to govern the development and use of military AI is crucial. This could include:
- (a) Establishing clear definitions and categories for autonomous weapons systems.
- (b) Setting limits on the level of autonomy permitted in weapons systems.
- (c) Creating verification and compliance mechanisms to ensure adherence to regulations.

(2) **Ethical guidelines and human control:** Implementing robust ethical frameworks and maintaining meaningful human control over AI systems is essential:
- (a) Developing clear ethical guidelines for the design and use of military AI.
- (b) Ensuring that humans remain “in the loop” for critical decisions, especially those involving the use of lethal force.
- (c) Implementing fail-safe mechanisms and human override capabilities in autonomous systems.

(3) **Transparency and confidence-building measures:** Promoting openness and trust between nations regarding military AI development:
- (a) Encouraging information sharing about AI capabilities and limitations.
- (b) Establishing international forums for dialogue on military AI issues.
- (c) Conducting joint exercises and simulations to build trust and understanding.

(4) **AI safety research:** Investing in research to ensure the reliability, robustness, and safety of military AI systems:
- (a) Developing rigorous testing and validation methodologies for AI systems.
- (b) Researching methods to make AI systems more explainable and interpretable.
- (c) Exploring techniques to make AI systems resilient to adversarial attacks and manipulation.

(5) **Non-proliferation efforts**: Preventing the spread of advanced military AI technologies to potentially destabilizing actors:
- (a) Implementing export controls on sensitive AI technologies and knowledge.
- (b) Strengthening international cooperation to prevent the illicit transfer of military AI capabilities.

   (c) Providing alternative technologies and development assistance to discourage the pursuit of military AI by some nations.

(6) **Capacity building and education:** Ensuring that military personnel, policymakers, and the public understand the implications of military AI:
   (a) Developing comprehensive education programs on AI for military leaders and personnel.
   (b) Promoting public awareness and debate on the ethical and security implications of military AI.
   (c) Fostering interdisciplinary collaboration between AI researchers, ethicists, and military strategists.

(7) **Crisis communication mechanisms:** Establishing robust communication channels to prevent misunderstandings and accidental escalation:
   (a) Creating hotlines and secure communication protocols specifically for AI-related incidents.
   (b) Developing shared protocols for de-escalation in case of AI system malfunctions or unexpected behaviors.
   (c) Conducting regular exercises to test and improve crisis communication procedures.

The integration of AI into military systems presents both unprecedented opportunities and significant challenges. While AI has the potential to enhance military capabilities, improve decision-making, and reduce human casualties, it also raises profound ethical, legal, and security concerns. The rapid pace of AI development in the military sphere necessitates urgent action to establish international norms, regulations, and safety measures. As we move forward, it is crucial to strike a balance between harnessing the benefits of military AI and mitigating its risks. This will require sustained international cooperation, robust governance frameworks, and a commitment to maintaining human control over critical decisions. By proactively addressing the challenges posed by military AI, we can work towards a future where technological advancements contribute to global security rather than undermining it.

CHAPTER

6

The Rise of Artificial Intelligence in Diplomacy and International Relations

DOI: 10.1201/9788743812937-6

In recent years, artificial intelligence (AI) has emerged as a transformative force across various sectors, and the realm of diplomacy and international relations is no exception. As nations grapple with increasingly complex global challenges, from climate change to cybersecurity threats, AI presents both opportunities and risks in the conduct of foreign affairs. This chapter explores the multifaceted impact of AI on diplomacy and international relations, examining its advantages, disadvantages, challenges, and potential future developments.

Figure 6.1 AI in diplomacy.

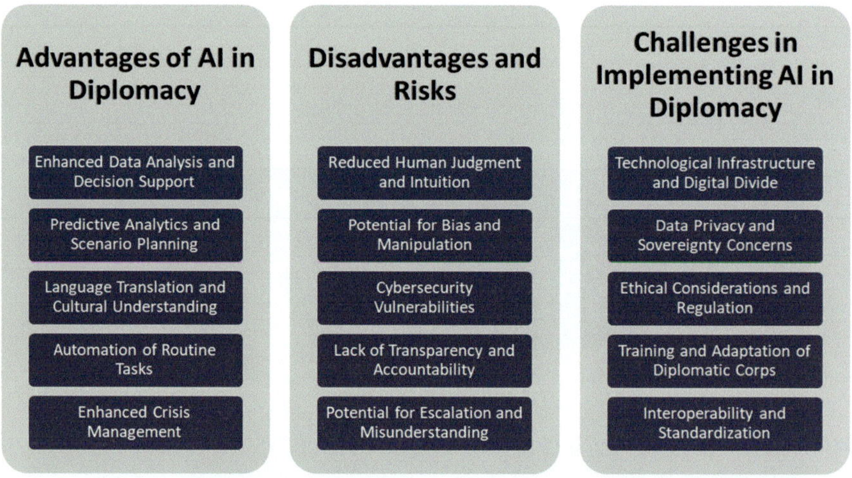

Advantages of AI in Diplomacy, Figure 6.1

(1) **Enhanced data analysis and decision support.** One of the most significant advantages of AI in diplomacy is its ability to process and analyze vast amounts of data quickly and efficiently. Diplomatic missions generate enormous quantities of information through reports, communications, and open-source intelligence. AI-powered systems can sift through this data, identifying patterns, trends, and insights that human analysts might overlook.

For example, machine learning algorithms can analyze historical diplomatic communications to identify subtle shifts in language or tone that may indicate changes in a nation's stance on particular issues. This capability allows diplomats to make more informed decisions and develop nuanced strategies based on comprehensive data analysis.

(2) **Predictive analytics and scenario planning.** AI's predictive capabilities offer valuable support for diplomatic planning and strategy development. By analyzing historical data and current trends, AI models can forecast potential outcomes of various diplomatic actions or geopolitical events. This enables diplomats to engage in more sophisticated scenario planning, anticipating possible consequences and preparing appropriate responses.

For instance, AI systems could model the potential economic and political impacts of proposed trade agreements, helping negotiators understand the long-term implications of different clauses or concessions. This foresight can lead to more balanced and sustainable international agreements.

(3) **Language translation and cultural understanding.** AI-powered language translation tools have significantly improved in recent years, breaking down language barriers in diplomatic communications. Real-time translation capabilities can facilitate more direct and nuanced conversations between diplomats from different linguistic backgrounds, reducing misunderstandings and fostering closer relationships.

Moreover, advanced natural language processing (NLP) models can analyze cultural context and idiomatic expressions, helping diplomats navigate the subtleties of cross-cultural communication. This enhanced understanding can lead to more effective negotiations and stronger international partnerships.

(4) **Automation of routine tasks.** AI can automate many routine diplomatic tasks, freeing up human diplomats to focus on high-level strategy and relationship-building. For example, AI systems can manage scheduling, draft routine correspondence, and compile regular reports on specific issues or regions. This automation can increase the overall efficiency of diplomatic missions and allow human diplomats to devote more time to complex problem-solving and critical negotiations.

(5) **Enhanced crisis management.** In times of international crisis, AI can provide rapid analysis of developing situations, helping diplomats respond quickly and effectively. Machine learning algorithms can monitor global news sources, social media, and other data streams to detect early warning signs of potential conflicts or humanitarian crises. This early detection can enable proactive diplomatic interventions, potentially prevent escalation or mitigate the impact of crises.

Disadvantages and Risks, Figure 6.1

(1) **Reduced human judgment and intuition.** While AI excels at data analysis and pattern recognition, it lacks the nuanced understanding and intuition that experienced human diplomats bring to their work. Diplomacy often requires a delicate touch, an understanding of historical and cultural contexts, and the ability to read between the lines in complex negotiations. Over-reliance on AI-generated insights could lead to oversimplified or misguided diplomatic strategies that fail to account for the full complexity of international relations.

(2) **Potential for bias and manipulation.** AI systems are only as unbiased as the data they are trained on and the algorithms that process that data. If diplomatic AI tools are developed using

biased historical data or flawed algorithms, they could perpetuate or even exacerbate existing prejudices and power imbalances in international relations. There is also the risk that bad actors could intentionally manipulate AI systems to skew diplomatic decision-making in their favor.

(3) **Cybersecurity vulnerabilities.** As diplomatic processes become increasingly reliant on AI and digital technologies, they also become more vulnerable to cyberattacks. Hostile actors could potentially hack AI systems to steal sensitive diplomatic information, manipulate data, or disrupt critical diplomatic communications. The integration of AI into diplomacy thus necessitates robust cybersecurity measures to protect the integrity and confidentiality of diplomatic processes.

(4) **Lack of transparency and accountability.** The complex nature of many AI algorithms, particularly deep learning models, can make it difficult to understand how they arrive at specific conclusions or recommendations. This "black box" problem could undermine trust in AI-assisted diplomatic decision-making and raise questions about accountability. If an AI system recommends a particular diplomatic action that leads to negative consequences, it may be challenging to determine responsibility and learn from the mistake.

(5) **Potential for escalation and misunderstanding.** In crisis situations, the speed and automation of AI-powered systems could potentially lead to rapid escalation of conflicts. If multiple nations employ AI for diplomatic decision-making, there is a risk of creating feedback loops where AI systems react to each other's outputs, potentially escalating tensions before human diplomats can intervene. Additionally, cultural nuances or contextual factors that a human diplomat might intuitively understand could be lost on an AI system, leading to misinterpretations or inappropriate responses.

Challenges in Implementing AI in Diplomacy, Figure 6.1

(1) **Technological infrastructure and digital divide.** Effective implementation of AI in diplomacy requires robust technological infrastructure and digital literacy. However, there is a significant digital divide between nations, with some countries lacking the necessary resources to develop or deploy advanced AI systems for diplomatic purposes. This disparity could exacerbate existing power imbalances in international relations, giving technologically advanced nations an unfair advantage in diplomatic negotiations and global decision-making processes.

(2) **Data privacy and sovereignty concerns.** The use of AI in diplomacy raises important questions about data privacy and national sovereignty. Diplomatic communications often contain sensitive information, and nations may be reluctant to share this data with AI systems, particularly if those systems are developed or hosted by other countries. Establishing international norms and agreements on the use of data in diplomatic AI applications will be crucial to address these concerns and build trust in AI-assisted diplomacy.

(3) **Ethical considerations and regulation.** As AI takes on a more prominent role in diplomacy, there is a need to develop ethical guidelines and regulatory frameworks to govern its use. Questions arise about the appropriate balance between human and AI decision-making

in diplomatic processes, the transparency of AI systems used in international relations, and the potential consequences of AI-driven diplomacy on global stability and human rights. Crafting international agreements on these issues will be challenging but necessary to ensure responsible use of AI in diplomacy.

(4) **Training and adaptation of diplomatic corps.** Integrating AI into diplomatic processes will require significant changes in how diplomats are trained and how diplomatic institutions operate. Diplomats will need to develop new skills to effectively work alongside AI systems, interpreting and applying AI-generated insights while maintaining their critical human judgment. Diplomatic academies and foreign ministries will need to adapt their curricula and operational procedures to prepare for an AI-augmented diplomatic landscape.

(5) **Interoperability and standardization.** As different nations develop their own AI systems for diplomatic purposes, ensuring interoperability between these systems will be crucial for effective international communication and cooperation. Establishing common standards and protocols for diplomatic AI applications will be a complex challenge, requiring extensive international collaboration and negotiation.

Future Prospects for AI in Diplomacy

(1) **AI-enhanced multilateral negotiations.** In the future, AI could play a significant role in facilitating complex multilateral negotiations on global issues such as climate change, trade, and disarmament. AI systems could analyze the positions and interests of multiple parties, identify potential areas of agreement, and suggest compromise solutions that maximize benefits for all stakeholders. This could lead to more efficient and effective international agreements on pressing global challenges.

(2) **Personalized diplomatic engagement.** Advanced AI systems could enable more personalized and targeted diplomatic engagement. By analyzing vast amounts of data on individual leaders, cultural contexts, and historical relationships, AI could help diplomats tailor their approach to specific counterparts or situations. This personalized diplomacy could lead to more productive interactions and stronger international relationships.

(3) **Virtual diplomatic presence.** As AI and virtual reality technologies advance, we may see the emergence of AI-powered virtual diplomats or digital embassies. These could provide a constant diplomatic presence in foreign countries, available 24/7 to answer questions, provide information, and facilitate cultural exchange. While not replacing human diplomats, these virtual presences could complement traditional diplomatic missions and expand a nation's soft power reach.

(4) **Predictive conflict resolution.** Future AI systems may be able to predict potential conflicts with a high degree of accuracy by analyzing a wide range of indicators, from economic data to social media sentiment. This predictive capability could enable more proactive diplomatic interventions to prevent conflicts before they escalate, potentially saving lives and promoting global stability.

(5) **AI-driven public diplomacy.** AI could revolutionize public diplomacy efforts by enabling more targeted and effective communication with foreign publics. Machine learning algorithms

could analyze public sentiment in real-time, allowing diplomats to adjust their messaging and engagement strategies dynamically. AI-powered chatbots and virtual assistants could also provide personalized information about a country's culture, policies, and values to interested individuals around the world.

(6) **Quantum computing and diplomatic simulations.** As quantum computing technology matures, it could dramatically enhance the capabilities of AI in diplomacy. Quantum-powered AI systems could run incredibly complex simulations of global events and diplomatic scenarios, providing insights and predictions at a level of detail and accuracy previously unimaginable. This could fundamentally change how nations approach strategic planning and diplomatic decision-making.

(7) **AI ethics in international relations.** As AI becomes more prevalent in diplomacy and international relations, we may see the emergence of new diplomatic roles focused on AI ethics and governance. Nations may appoint AI ambassadors or establish international bodies dedicated to developing global norms and regulations for the use of AI in diplomacy and other aspects of international affairs.

The integration of AI into diplomacy and international relations presents a complex landscape of opportunities and challenges. While AI offers significant advantages in terms of data analysis, predictive capabilities, and efficiency, it also raises important concerns about human judgment, bias, security, and ethical implications.

As we move forward, it will be crucial for nations to collaborate on developing ethical guidelines, regulatory frameworks, and best practices for the use of AI in diplomacy. The goal should be to harness the power of AI to enhance human diplomatic efforts, rather than to replace human diplomats entirely. By striking the right balance between AI capabilities and human expertise, we can work towards a future where technology supports more effective, informed, and peaceful international relations.

Ultimately, the successful integration of AI into diplomacy will require ongoing dialogue, adaptation, and cooperation among nations. As AI continues to evolve, so too must our approach to its use in the delicate and critical realm of international diplomacy. By addressing the challenges head-on and thoughtfully leveraging the advantages of AI, we can strive for a more connected, stable, and prosperous global community.

CHAPTER

7

Artificial Intelligence and National Security

DOI: 10.1201/9788743812937-7

In the rapidly evolving landscape of global security, artificial intelligence (AI) has emerged as a transformative force, reshaping the way nations approach defense, intelligence, and strategic planning. As countries around the world invest heavily in AI technologies, the implications for national security are profound and far-reaching. This chapter explores the multifaceted impact of AI on national security, examining its advantages, disadvantages, challenges, and potential future developments.

Figure 7.1 AI in national security.

Advantages of AI in National Security	Disadvantages and Risks	Challenges in Implementing AI for National Security
• Enhanced Intelligence Gathering and Analysis • Predictive Analytics and Threat Assessment • Cybersecurity and Network Defense • Autonomous and Semi-Autonomous Systems • Decision Support in Crisis Situations	• Vulnerability to Adversarial Attacks • Potential for Autonomous Weapons Systems • Over-reliance on AI and Erosion of Human Expertise • Data Privacy and Civil Liberties Concerns • Potential for Escalation and Misunderstanding	• Ethical and Legal Frameworks • Data Quality and Bias • Interoperability and Standardization • Workforce Development and Adaptation • Adversarial AI and the AI Arms Race • Explainability and Transparency

Advantages of AI in National Security, Figure 7.1

(1) **Enhanced intelligence gathering and analysis.** One of the most significant advantages of AI in national security is its ability to process and analyze vast amounts of data quickly and efficiently. Intelligence agencies generate enormous quantities of information from various sources, including satellite imagery, communications intercepts, and open-source intelligence. AI-powered systems can sift through this data, identifying patterns, anomalies, and potential threats that human analysts might miss.

For example, machine learning algorithms can analyze satellite images to detect changes in military installations or unusual troop movements. Natural language processing (NLP) models can scan millions of social media posts to identify emerging security threats or track the spread of disinformation campaigns. This enhanced analytical capability allows security agencies to make more informed decisions and respond more quickly to potential threats.

(2) **Predictive analytics and threat assessment.** AI's predictive capabilities offer valuable support for national security planning and strategy development. By analyzing historical data and current trends, AI models can forecast potential security risks, geopolitical developments, and emerging threats. This enables security agencies to engage in more sophisticated scenario planning, anticipating possible attacks or crises and preparing appropriate responses.

For instance, AI systems could model the potential impact of various factors—such as economic instability, climate change, or political unrest—on regional security, helping policymakers develop more effective long-term security strategies.

(3) **Cybersecurity and network defense.** As cyber threats become increasingly sophisticated, AI plays a crucial role in defending critical infrastructure and sensitive networks. Machine learning algorithms can monitor network traffic in real-time, detecting anomalies and potential intrusions far more quickly and accurately than traditional security systems. AI-powered threat intelligence platforms can analyze global cyber threat data to predict and prevent future attacks.

Moreover, AI can automate many aspects of cybersecurity, such as patch management and vulnerability assessment, reducing the workload on human security teams and allowing them to focus on more complex security challenges.

(4) **Autonomous and semi-autonomous systems.** AI enables the development of autonomous and semi-autonomous systems that can operate in environments too dangerous or inaccessible for humans. This includes unmanned aerial vehicles (UAVs) for reconnaissance and surveillance, autonomous underwater vehicles for naval operations, and robotic systems for explosive ordnance disposal.

These AI-powered systems can enhance military capabilities while reducing risks to human personnel. They can also operate for extended periods in harsh environments, providing persistent surveillance and intelligence gathering capabilities.

(5) **Decision support in crisis situations.** In times of crisis or conflict, AI can provide rapid analysis of developing situations, helping military and political leaders make informed decisions under pressure. Machine learning algorithms can process real-time data from multiple sources, providing a comprehensive picture of the battlefield or crisis zone. This can lead to more effective tactical decisions and potentially reduce casualties.

Disadvantages and Risks, Figure 7.1

(1) **Vulnerability to adversarial attacks.** While AI systems can enhance cybersecurity, they are also vulnerable to sophisticated adversarial attacks. Malicious actors can potentially manipulate the input data or exploit weaknesses in AI algorithms to deceive these systems. For example, subtle alterations to images could fool AI-powered surveillance systems, or carefully crafted text could bypass AI content filters.

This vulnerability could lead to serious security breaches or misinformation campaigns that undermine national security efforts.

(2) **Potential for autonomous weapons systems.** The development of fully autonomous weapons systems, often referred to as "killer robots," raises significant ethical and security concerns. These AI-powered systems could potentially select and engage targets without meaningful human control, raising questions about accountability and the potential for unintended escalation of conflicts.

The prospect of autonomous weapons systems also creates new arms race dynamics, as nations compete to develop increasingly sophisticated AI-powered military technologies.

(3) **Over-reliance on AI and erosion of human expertise.** As AI systems become more capable, there's a risk that security agencies may become overly reliant on these technologies, potentially eroding human expertise and judgment. Critical thinking, intuition, and the ability to understand complex geopolitical contexts are uniquely human skills that remain crucial in national security decision-making.

Over-dependence on AI could lead to a false sense of security or blind spots in threat assessment if the AI systems fail to account for novel or unprecedented scenarios.

(4) **Data privacy and civil liberties concerns.** The use of AI in national security often involves processing vast amounts of data, including information about citizens. This raises significant concerns about data privacy and civil liberties. The powerful surveillance capabilities enabled by AI could potentially be misused for political control or suppression of dissent, particularly in authoritarian regimes.

Balancing national security needs with individual privacy rights will be an ongoing challenge as AI technologies become more pervasive.

(5) **Potential for escalation and misunderstanding.** In crisis situations, the speed and automation of AI-powered systems could potentially lead to rapid escalation of conflicts. If multiple nations employ AI for military decision-making, there is a risk of creating feedback loops where AI systems react to each other's outputs, potentially escalating tensions before human leaders can intervene.

Additionally, the "black box" nature of some AI algorithms could make it difficult to understand how they arrive at specific recommendations, potentially leading to misunderstandings or mistrust between nations.

Challenges in Implementing AI for National Security, Figure 7.1

(1) **Ethical and legal frameworks.** The rapid advancement of AI in national security outpaces existing ethical and legal frameworks. Developing comprehensive guidelines for the responsible use of AI in defense and intelligence operations is a complex challenge. Questions arise about the appropriate level of human control over AI systems, the accountability for AI-driven decisions, and the potential consequences of AI-powered security operations on human rights and international law.

(2) **Data quality and bias.** The effectiveness of AI systems in national security depends heavily on the quality and representativeness of the data they are trained on. Biased or incomplete

data could lead to flawed analysis and potentially discriminatory outcomes. Ensuring that AI systems have access to high-quality, diverse, and unbiased data sets is a significant challenge, particularly given the sensitive nature of much national security information.

(3) **Interoperability and standardization.** As different agencies and allied nations develop their own AI systems for security purposes, ensuring interoperability between these systems becomes crucial. Establishing common standards and protocols for AI in national security applications will require extensive international collaboration and negotiation.

(4) **Workforce development and adaptation.** Integrating AI into national security operations requires a workforce with new skill sets. Security agencies need personnel who can develop, deploy, and interpret AI systems while also understanding the broader strategic and operational contexts. Recruiting and training this new generation of security professionals presents a significant challenge.

(5) **Adversarial AI and the AI arms race.** As nations invest in AI for national security, they must also prepare for adversaries using similar technologies. This creates a new dimension of competition, where countries race to develop more advanced AI capabilities while also working to defend against and potentially exploit weaknesses in adversaries' AI systems.

(6) **Explainability and transparency.** Many advanced AI systems, particularly deep learning models, operate as "black boxes," making it difficult to understand how they arrive at specific conclusions or recommendations. In the context of national security, where decisions can have life-or-death consequences, the lack of explainability in AI systems poses significant challenges. Developing AI models that can provide clear explanations for their outputs while maintaining their predictive power is an ongoing area of research.

Future Prospects for AI in National Security

(1) **Quantum AI and cryptography.** As quantum computing technology matures, it could dramatically enhance the capabilities of AI in national security. Quantum-powered AI systems could break current encryption methods, necessitating the development of new quantum-resistant cryptography. Conversely, quantum AI could also enable unbreakable encryption methods, revolutionizing secure communications for intelligence and military operations.

(2) **AI-enhanced wargaming and simulation.** Advanced AI systems could transform military planning and training through highly sophisticated wargaming and simulation capabilities. These systems could model complex geopolitical scenarios, allowing military strategists to test various approaches and better prepare for a wide range of potential conflicts or crises.

(3) **Cognitive electronic warfare.** AI is likely to play an increasingly important role in electronic warfare. AI-powered systems could engage in real-time spectrum analysis, rapidly identifying and countering enemy communications and radar systems. This could lead to a new era of cognitive electronic warfare, where AI systems engage in complex, dynamic electromagnetic battles.

(4) **Swarm intelligence and coordinated autonomous systems.** Future military operations may involve large swarms of autonomous drones or robots coordinated by AI systems. These swarms could perform complex tasks such as reconnaissance, area denial, or even coordinated attacks, presenting new challenges and opportunities for military strategists.

(5) **AI-driven threat prediction and prevention.** As AI systems become more sophisticated, they may be able to predict potential security threats with unprecedented accuracy. By analyzing vast amounts of data from diverse sources, AI could identify early warning signs of terrorist activities, cyber attacks, or geopolitical crises, allowing for more proactive security measures.

(6) **Human–AI teaming.** The future of national security is likely to involve close collaboration between human operators and AI systems. This could include AI-enhanced decision support systems for commanders, AI co-pilots for fighter jets, or AI assistants for intelligence analysts. Developing effective human–AI teaming protocols and interfaces will be a key area of focus.

(7) **AI ethics and international cooperation.** As AI becomes more central to national security, we may see the emergence of new international bodies and agreements focused on AI governance in defense and intelligence. This could include treaties on the use of AI in warfare, similar to existing arms control agreements, as well as collaborative efforts to address global security challenges using AI.

The integration of AI into national security presents a complex landscape of opportunities and challenges. While AI offers significant advantages in terms of data analysis, predictive capabilities, and enhanced defense systems, it also raises important concerns about ethics, privacy, and the potential for unintended escalation of conflicts.

As we move forward, it will be crucial for nations to collaborate on developing ethical guidelines, regulatory frameworks, and best practices for the use of AI in national security. The goal should be to harness the power of AI to enhance security and stability while mitigating risks and preserving human rights and international law.

Balancing the potential of AI with its risks will require ongoing dialogue, adaptation, and cooperation among nations. As AI continues to evolve, so too must our approach to its use in the critical domain of national security. By addressing the challenges head-on and thoughtfully leveraging the advantages of AI, we can strive for a safer and more stable global environment.

CHAPTER

8

AI and Higher Education: Transforming the Academic Landscape

Artificial intelligence (AI) is rapidly transforming various sectors of society, and higher education is no exception. As AI technologies continue to advance, they are reshaping the way we teach, learn, and conduct research in academic institutions. We will explore the multifaceted impact of AI on higher education, examining its advantages, disadvantages, challenges, potential, and future prospects.

DOI: 10.1201/9788743812937-8

Figure 8.1 AI in higher education.

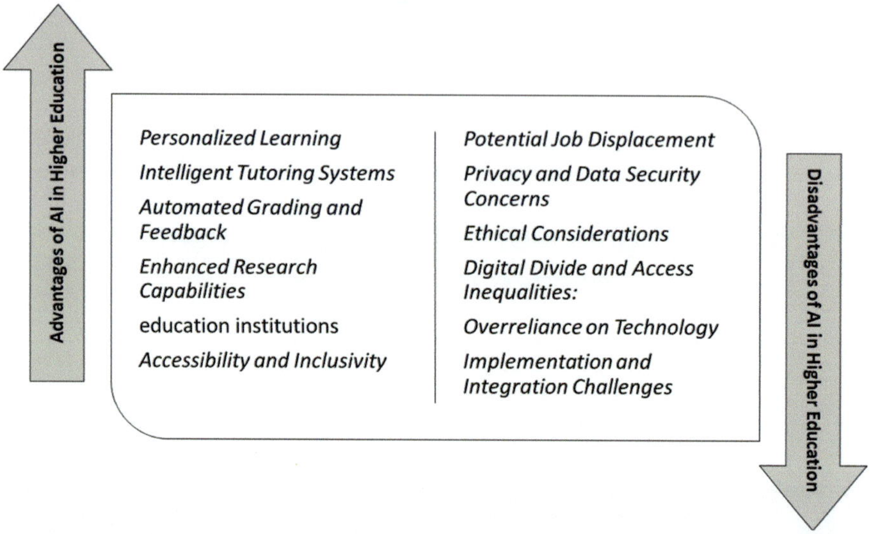

Advantages of AI in Higher Education

(1) **Personalized learning.** One of the most significant advantages of AI in higher education is its ability to provide personalized learning experiences. AI-powered adaptive learning systems can analyze individual student performance, learning styles, and preferences to tailor educational content and pacing. This personalization helps students learn more effectively and efficiently, addressing their specific needs and challenges (Figure 8.1).

(2) **Intelligent tutoring systems.** AI-driven tutoring systems can provide students with instant feedback and support, available 24/7. These systems can answer questions, explain concepts, and offer guidance, supplementing traditional instructor support. This constant availability of assistance can significantly enhance the learning process and reduce the burden on human educators.

(3) **Automated grading and feedback.** AI can automate the grading process for certain types of assignments, such as multiple-choice tests and short-answer questions. This not only saves time for instructors but also provides students with immediate feedback. Advanced AI systems can even evaluate essays and provide detailed feedback on writing style, structure, and content.

(4) **Enhanced research capabilities.** AI tools can significantly boost research capabilities in higher education. They can analyze vast amounts of data, identify patterns, and generate insights that might be difficult for humans to discover. This can accelerate scientific discoveries and contribute to more efficient and effective research processes across various disciplines.

(5) **Improved administrative efficiency.** AI can streamline administrative tasks in higher education institutions. From managing enrollment and scheduling to handling student inquiries and processing financial aid applications, AI can increase efficiency and reduce human error in various administrative processes.

(6) **Accessibility and inclusivity.** AI-powered tools can enhance accessibility in higher education. For instance, real-time speech-to-text conversion can assist hearing-impaired students, while AI-driven language translation can support international students. These technologies can make education more inclusive and accessible to diverse student populations.

Disadvantages of AI in Higher Education, Figure 8.1

(1) **Potential job displacement.** As AI takes over certain tasks traditionally performed by humans, there are concerns about potential job displacement in higher education. Some administrative roles and even certain teaching positions might be at risk of being automated, leading to workforce challenges within academic institutions.

(2) **Privacy and data security concerns.** The use of AI in education involves collecting and analyzing large amounts of student data. This raises significant privacy and data security concerns. Institutions must ensure robust data protection measures and comply with relevant regulations to safeguard sensitive student information.

(3) **Ethical considerations.** The use of AI in decision-making processes, such as admissions or grading, raises ethical questions. There are concerns about potential bias in AI algorithms and the fairness of AI-driven decisions. Ensuring transparency and accountability in AI systems is crucial to maintain trust in educational processes.

(4) **Digital divide and access inequalities.** The implementation of AI technologies in higher education may exacerbate existing digital divides. Students and institutions with limited access to advanced technologies or high-speed internet may be at a disadvantage, potentially widening educational inequalities.

(5) **Overreliance on technology.** There is a risk of overreliance on AI technologies in education. This could potentially lead to a decrease in critical thinking skills and human interaction, which are crucial aspects of the educational experience. Striking a balance between AI-assisted learning and traditional human-led instruction is essential.

(6) **Implementation and integration challenges.** Integrating AI systems into existing educational infrastructures can be complex and costly. Many institutions may face challenges in terms of technical implementation, staff training, and adapting curricula to incorporate AI technologies effectively.

Potential of AI in Higher Education

(1) **Hyper-personalized learning pathways.** The future of AI in higher education points towards even more sophisticated personalization. AI could create hyper-personalized learning

pathways that adapt not just to a student's academic performance, but also to their career goals, personal interests, and even real-time emotional states. This level of customization could revolutionize the concept of a "degree program," making education more relevant and engaging for each individual student.

(2) **AI-enhanced virtual and augmented reality.** The integration of AI with virtual and augmented reality technologies holds immense potential for higher education. AI-driven VR and AR experiences could provide immersive learning environments, allowing students to interact with complex concepts in a 3D space. For instance, medical students could practice surgeries in virtual environments, while history students could "walk through" accurately recreated historical settings.

(3) **Predictive analytics for student success.** AI's predictive capabilities could be harnessed to identify students at risk of dropping out or struggling academically. By analyzing patterns in student data, AI systems could alert advisors and instructors early on, enabling timely interventions and support. This proactive approach could significantly improve retention rates and overall student success.

(4) **AI-powered research assistants.** Future AI systems could serve as sophisticated research assistants, not just in data analysis but in hypothesis generation and experimental design. These AI assistants could help researchers explore new avenues of inquiry, cross-pollinate ideas from different disciplines, and accelerate the pace of scientific discovery.

(5) **Continuous learning and skill adaptation.** As the job market evolves rapidly, AI could play a crucial role in helping higher education institutions adapt their curricula in real-time. By analyzing job market trends and skill demands, AI systems could suggest curriculum updates, ensuring that education remains relevant to the changing needs of the workforce.

(6) **Global collaboration and knowledge sharing.** AI could facilitate unprecedented levels of global collaboration in higher education. Language barriers could be overcome with real-time AI translation, allowing students and researchers from different parts of the world to collaborate seamlessly. AI could also help in creating and managing vast, interconnected knowledge networks, making the collective wisdom of academia more accessible than ever before.

Challenges and Considerations

(1) **Maintaining the human element.** As AI becomes more prevalent in higher education, maintaining the crucial human elements of teaching and learning will be a significant challenge. The mentorship, empathy, and inspiration that human educators provide cannot be fully replicated by AI. Finding the right balance between AI-assisted education and human interaction will be key to preserving the holistic nature of higher education.

(2) **Ethical AI development and implementation.** Ensuring that AI systems in education are developed and implemented ethically will be an ongoing challenge. This includes addressing

issues of bias, fairness, and transparency in AI algorithms. Higher education institutions will need to establish clear ethical guidelines and governance structures for AI use.

(3) **Adapting pedagogical approaches.** The integration of AI will necessitate a rethinking of traditional pedagogical approaches. Educators will need to adapt their teaching methods to effectively leverage AI tools while fostering critical thinking, creativity, and social skills that remain uniquely human.

(4) **Bridging the digital divide.** As AI becomes more integral to higher education, addressing the digital divide will be crucial. Ensuring equitable access to AI-enhanced education across different socioeconomic backgrounds and geographical regions will be a significant challenge that requires concerted effort from institutions, governments, and technology providers.

(5) **Lifelong learning and continuous education.** The rapid pace of technological change means that the concept of education as a one-time event early in life is becoming obsolete. Higher education institutions will need to evolve to support lifelong learning, potentially using AI to create flexible, modular education systems that allow individuals to continually update their skills throughout their careers.

(6) **Data privacy and security.** As AI systems in education become more sophisticated and collect more data, ensuring the privacy and security of this information will be paramount. Institutions will need to invest in robust cybersecurity measures and navigate complex data protection regulations.

The Future of AI in Higher Education

The integration of AI in higher education presents a landscape rich with opportunities and challenges. While AI has the potential to *revolutionize learning experiences, enhance research capabilities, and improve administrative efficiency, it also brings concerns about job displacement, privacy, and the preservation of essential human elements in education.*

The future of AI in higher education is likely to see even more personalized and immersive learning experiences, AI-assisted research breakthroughs, and a shift towards more flexible, lifelong learning models. However, realizing this potential will require careful navigation of ethical, technological, and pedagogical challenges.

As we move forward, it will be crucial for higher education institutions, policymakers, and technology developers to *work collaboratively*. They must ensure that AI is implemented in ways that enhance rather than diminish the quality and accessibility of education. The goal should be to harness the power of AI to create more effective, equitable, and engaging learning environments while preserving the core values and human-centric aspects of higher education.

Ultimately, the successful integration of AI in higher education will depend on our ability to view AI not as a replacement for human intelligence and interaction, but as a *powerful tool* to augment and enhance the educational experience. By striking the right balance, we can create a future of higher education that is more personalized, accessible, and effective, preparing students for a world where human creativity and AI capabilities work in harmony.

CHAPTER

9

The Use of AI in the Criminal Justice Field

DOI: 10.1201/9788743812937-9

Artificial intelligence (AI) has revolutionized various sectors, including healthcare, finance, and education. One of the most transformative impacts of AI, however, is in the criminal justice field. From predictive policing to the analysis of court transcripts, AI technologies are being deployed to enhance the efficiency, accuracy, and fairness of criminal justice processes.

The Evolution of AI in Criminal Justice

The integration of AI into criminal justice began with the development of basic data analysis tools that assisted law enforcement agencies in identifying crime patterns. Over time, advancements in machine learning, natural language processing, and big data analytics have led to more sophisticated applications (Figure 9.1).

Today, AI is utilized in various aspects of criminal justice, including:

- **Predictive policing:** Using data-driven algorithms to forecast criminal activities and deploy resources efficiently.
- **Facial recognition:** Identifying suspects and missing persons through advanced image processing techniques.
- **Risk assessment tools:** Evaluating the likelihood of re-offending to inform bail and sentencing decisions.
- **Automated case management:** Streamlining administrative tasks in legal proceedings.

Predictive Policing

How it works: Predictive policing involves the use of AI algorithms to analyze historical crime data and predict future incidents. These algorithms can identify hotspots for criminal activity, allowing law enforcement agencies to allocate resources more effectively.

Benefits:

- **Resource optimization:** Enables efficient deployment of police forces.
- **Crime prevention:** Helps in preventing crimes by increasing police presence in predicted hot-spots.
- **Data-driven decisions:** Reduces reliance on subjective judgment, promoting objective decision-making.

Figure 9.1 AI in criminal justice.

Challenges and criticisms:

- **Bias in data:** AI systems can perpetuate existing biases present in historical crime data, leading to disproportionate targeting of certain communities.
- **Privacy concerns:** Increased surveillance and data collection can infringe on individual privacy rights.
- **Reliability issues:** Predictions are not foolproof and can lead to false positives.

Facial Recognition

Technology overview: Facial recognition technology uses AI to match facial features from images or video footage with databases of known faces. This technology is widely used for identifying suspects, verifying identities, and locating missing persons.

Applications in criminal justice:

- **Surveillance:** Monitoring public spaces for known offenders.
- **Investigation:** Assisting in the identification of suspects from security camera footage.
- **Security:** Enhancing security measures in courts and correctional facilities.

Ethical and legal concerns:

- **Accuracy and bias:** Facial recognition systems can exhibit bias, particularly against minority groups, leading to wrongful identifications.
- **Regulation:** There is a need for stringent regulations to govern the use of facial recognition technology to prevent misuse.
- **Consent and privacy:** The use of this technology often raises issues regarding consent and the right to privacy.

Risk Assessment Tools

Purpose and functionality: Risk assessment tools use AI to evaluate the risk of reoffending, which informs decisions regarding bail, sentencing, and parole. These tools analyze various factors, including criminal history, socioeconomic status, and psychological profiles.

Advantages:

- **Informed decision-making:** Provides judges and parole boards with data-driven insights.
- **Consistency:** Promotes consistency in judicial decisions, reducing disparities.
- **Efficiency:** Streamlines the decision-making process, saving time and resources.

Limitations:

- **Bias and fairness:** These tools can inherit biases from the data they are trained on, potentially leading to unfair outcomes.
- **Transparency:** The proprietary nature of many algorithms means their inner workings are not always transparent.
- **Dependence on data quality:** The accuracy of predictions is heavily reliant on the quality and completeness of the input data.

Automated Case Management

Streamlining legal processes: AI-driven case management systems automate various administrative tasks, such as scheduling, document management, and workflow coordination. These systems improve the efficiency and effectiveness of legal processes.

Benefits:

- **Time savings:** Reduces the administrative burden on legal professionals.
- **Accuracy:** Minimizes human errors in document handling and case tracking.
- **Accessibility:** Improves access to case information for all stakeholders.

Implementation challenges:

- **Integration with existing systems:** Ensuring compatibility with legacy systems can be complex.
- **User training:** Requires training for legal professionals to effectively use new technologies.
- **Data security:** Protecting sensitive legal information from cyber threats is paramount.

AI in Court Proceedings

- **AI-powered legal research:** AI tools can rapidly analyze vast amounts of legal documents and case law to provide relevant information, aiding lawyers in case preparation and research.
- **Predictive analytics in litigation:** AI can predict the likely outcomes of litigation based on historical data, helping legal teams to strategize effectively.
- **Virtual legal assistants:** AI-driven virtual assistants can support lawyers by managing schedules, sending reminders, and even drafting basic legal documents.

Ethical and Social Implications

- **Ensuring fairness and equity:** The deployment of AI in criminal justice must be guided by principles of fairness and equity. Addressing biases in AI systems is critical to prevent the perpetuation of existing inequalities.

- **Transparency and accountability:** Transparency in AI algorithms and accountability for their decisions are essential. Stakeholders must understand how decisions are made and have recourse in cases of errors or biases.
- Public trust and acceptance: Building public trust in AI technologies involves engaging with communities, being transparent about the use of AI, and ensuring that these technologies are used ethically.

Future Directions

- **Advancements in AI technology:** Continued advancements in AI, such as improved natural language processing and machine learning techniques, will enhance the capabilities of AI systems in criminal justice.
- **Policy and regulation:** Developing comprehensive policies and regulations to govern the use of AI in criminal justice is crucial. These regulations should address issues of fairness, transparency, and accountability.
- **Collaboration and research:** Collaboration between law enforcement agencies, legal professionals, technologists, and researchers will be essential to ensure that AI is used effectively and ethically in criminal justice.

AI has the potential to transform the criminal justice field by enhancing efficiency, accuracy, and fairness. However, it also raises significant ethical and social challenges. Ensuring that AI systems are designed and used responsibly will be key to realizing their benefits while minimizing their risks. By addressing issues of bias, transparency, and accountability, we can harness the power of AI to create a more just and equitable criminal justice system.

CHAPTER 10

AI in the Medical Field: Transforming Healthcare for the Future

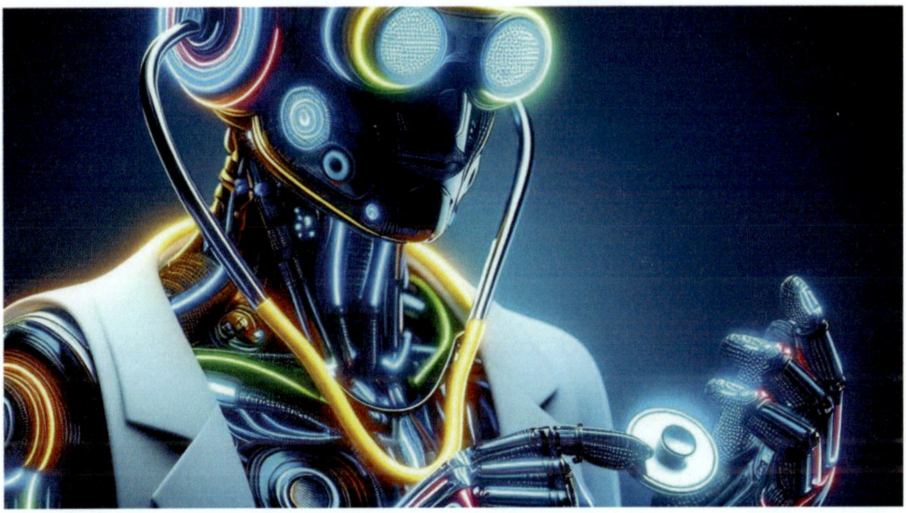

Artificial intelligence (AI) is revolutionizing industries worldwide, and the medical field is no exception. From diagnostics to treatment, AI is making profound changes in how healthcare professionals deliver care, increasing efficiency, reducing errors, and ultimately improving patient outcomes. We will explore AI's applications in healthcare, its advantages and challenges, ethical considerations, and what the future may hold.

DOI: 10.1201/9788743812937-10

Figure 10.1 AI and the medical field.

The Intersection of AI and Healthcare

The integration of AI into healthcare marks a significant paradigm shift, driven by advancements in machine learning (ML), natural language processing (NLP), and big data analytics. AI's ability to analyze complex data sets, detect patterns, and offer insights faster than humans has made it indispensable in diagnostics, personalized medicine, surgical assistance, and patient management.

For decades, healthcare has relied on human expertise and traditional tools. However, with the exponential growth in medical data and complexity of healthcare needs, it has become nearly impossible for human practitioners to keep up without assistance. AI technologies offer a solution by helping clinicians make faster and more accurate decisions (Figure 10.1).

AI applications in medical diagnostics: AI's potential to improve diagnostics is one of its most significant contributions to the medical field. Medical imaging, pathology, and genomics have particularly benefited from AI algorithms.

Medical imaging: AI in medical imaging has made it possible to detect diseases like cancer, heart disease, and neurological disorders more accurately and at earlier stages. Algorithms can analyze X-rays, CT scans, MRIs, and ultrasounds to identify abnormalities that may be too subtle for the human eye to catch. For instance, AI has shown to be particularly effective in identifying breast cancer in mammograms, sometimes outperforming human radiologists.

AI-powered image recognition tools also assist in diagnosing brain injuries, lung diseases, and fractures. These tools can process large volumes of images in seconds, enabling quicker diagnoses in emergency settings, which can be life-saving.

Pathology and lab tests: In pathology, AI is used to analyze tissue samples and detect cancerous cells or other abnormalities. Machine learning models can detect patterns and classify diseases more efficiently than traditional methods. This allows for faster diagnoses and reduces the likelihood of human error, especially in complex or rare conditions.

In the field of laboratory medicine, AI algorithms have been applied to automate the interpretation of test results. This has greatly enhanced the speed and accuracy of blood tests, genetic analysis, and other diagnostic procedures.

Personalized medicine and AI: Personalized medicine is an emerging field where AI plays a crucial role by tailoring treatments to individual patients based on their genetic makeup, lifestyle, and other factors. AI can analyze a patient's genetic data and predict their response to various drugs or treatments, ensuring a more personalized and effective approach.

Pharmacogenomics: AI assists in the field of pharmacogenomics, where machine learning algorithms predict how different patients will respond to drugs based on their genetic profiles. This allows healthcare providers to design tailored treatment plans, avoiding adverse drug reactions and optimizing dosages.

Predictive analytics: Predictive analytics powered by AI can foresee disease risks in patients before symptoms appear. This is especially useful in chronic diseases like diabetes, heart disease, and certain cancers, where early detection is crucial for effective intervention. AI models analyze vast amounts of health data, including patient history, genetic information, and lifestyle factors, to predict the likelihood of future health issues.

AI in surgery and robotic assistance: AI-powered robotic systems have made significant strides in the field of surgery, allowing for greater precision, less invasive procedures, and faster recovery times.

Robotic surgery: AI-enhanced robotic systems such assist surgeons in performing complex procedures with precision that would be difficult to achieve with human hands alone. These systems provide high-definition, 3D views of the surgical site and allow for minimally invasive procedures, which reduce recovery time and minimize risks of complications.

Autonomous surgical systems: AI is also moving toward fully autonomous surgical systems that can perform certain tasks independently. These systems rely on algorithms to make decisions during surgery, adjusting to the patient's specific needs in real-time. While still in the experimental phase, such systems represent the next frontier in AI-driven healthcare.

AI in drug discovery: The process of discovering new drugs is costly and time-consuming, often taking years and billions of dollars to bring a new drug to market. AI has the potential to transform this process by speeding up the identification of potential drug candidates, optimizing clinical trials, and predicting success rates.

Drug development: AI algorithms analyze vast datasets from clinical trials, medical literature, and genetic information to identify compounds that could be effective against particular diseases. AI-driven platforms use deep learning to predict how drugs will interact with the human body, significantly accelerating the drug discovery process.

Clinical trials: AI is also improving the efficiency of clinical trials by helping researchers select ideal candidates for testing and predicting how different groups of patients will respond to a treatment. This can significantly shorten the time it takes to bring new drugs to market.

AI in patient care and monitoring: AI is transforming patient care beyond diagnosis and treatment by improving monitoring and management, especially for chronic diseases.

Virtual health assistants: AI-powered virtual assistants, like chat-bots, help patients manage their conditions by providing timely reminders, answering questions, and tracking symptoms. These tools are particularly valuable in managing chronic diseases such as diabetes, hypertension, and asthma. Virtual health assistants can monitor patients' vital signs through wearable devices and provide real-time feedback, alerting healthcare providers when intervention is needed.

Remote monitoring: AI enhances remote monitoring technologies, allowing healthcare providers to keep track of patients outside of traditional healthcare settings. AI-driven devices collect and analyze data from wearable sensors, such as heart rate monitors or glucose meters, ensuring continuous patient care. These devices help detect early warning signs of health issues, leading to prompt interventions and reducing hospital re-admissions.

AI and electronic health records (EHRs): Electronic health records (EHRs) have long been a cornerstone of digital healthcare, but managing and extracting useful insights from EHR data is a challenge. AI has the potential to make EHRs more intelligent, efficient, and useful for both patients and healthcare providers.

Data extraction and analysis: AI tools can automatically extract relevant information from EHRs, such as patient history, laboratory results, and treatment plans, making it easier for healthcare providers to get a comprehensive view of a patient's health. These AI systems reduce administrative burdens on healthcare workers and ensure that they have the most relevant information when making clinical decisions.

Predictive analysis in EHRs: Predictive analytics within EHR systems is a growing trend, where AI models analyze patient data to predict potential complications or risks. For example, AI can identify patients at high risk for sepsis, a life-threatening condition, before symptoms become apparent. This allows for preemptive treatments, potentially saving lives.

The ethical and legal considerations of AI in healthcare: While AI holds enormous promise, its integration into healthcare also brings ethical and legal challenges that must be addressed. Issues around patient data privacy, algorithmic bias, and the role of AI in decision-making are at the forefront of the discussion.

Privacy concerns: AI systems rely on vast amounts of personal health data, raising concerns about how this data is collected, stored, and used. The misuse of sensitive patient information could lead to breaches of privacy and trust. Healthcare providers and AI developers must ensure that data security measures are robust, and patients are informed about how their data is being utilized.

Bias in AI algorithms: Bias in AI algorithms is a critical issue, particularly in healthcare, where the consequences of biased decisions can be life-threatening. If AI models are trained on data that under-represents certain populations, they may fail to provide accurate diagnoses or treatment recommendations for these groups. Developers must work to ensure that AI systems are trained on diverse datasets to mitigate this risk.

Accountability and liability: The question of accountability in AI-driven healthcare decisions is complex. Who is responsible if an AI system makes a mistake—the developers, the healthcare provider, or the hospital? Legal frameworks are still catching up to these issues, and clarity is needed on liability and accountability for AI-related errors in medical care.

The future of AI in healthcare: The future of AI in healthcare is full of potential. As AI technologies continue to improve, we can expect even more advanced applications, such as AI-driven preventive care, more sophisticated surgical robots, and AI-based treatment planning for complex diseases like cancer.

AI in preventive medicine: AI's ability to predict disease onset and progression will drive the future of preventive medicine. By analyzing genetic, environmental, and lifestyle data, AI will enable healthcare providers to offer tailored preventive measures for patients, reducing the burden of chronic diseases and enhancing overall public health.

AI and genomics: The combination of AI and genomics will likely lead to groundbreaking discoveries in personalized medicine. AI can rapidly analyze genetic information, providing insights into individual disease risks and helping to design targeted treatments. This could revolutionize treatments for complex conditions like cancer, where precision medicine is key.

Fully automated surgeries: Looking forward, AI systems may evolve to a point where fully autonomous surgeries are commonplace. These surgeries could be performed with high precision, minimizing human error and allowing surgeons to focus on more complex decision-making tasks.

AI is already reshaping the medical field in profound ways, and its potential is only just beginning to be realized. From enhancing diagnostics and treatment options to personalizing patient care and improving healthcare administration, AI offers unparalleled opportunities to improve patient outcomes. However, the medical community must navigate ethical, legal, and technical challenges to ensure that AI is used responsibly and effectively. As AI technologies continue to evolve, healthcare providers, policymakers, and technologists must collaborate to harness the full potential of AI while safeguarding patient rights, privacy, and safety. The future of healthcare is undoubtedly intertwined with the future of AI, and the possibilities are boundless.

CHAPTER

11

The Impact of Artificial Intelligence on Space Technology: Present Innovations and Future Trajectories

DOI: 10.1201/9788743812937-11

The fusion of artificial intelligence (AI) and space technology marks a revolutionary shift in our approach to space exploration, research, and commercialization. From autonomous navigation on Mars to real-time data analysis aboard satellites, AI is becoming an indispensable tool in the vast domain of space science. As the complexity and volume of data in space missions grow exponentially, AI's capacity to simulate intelligence, process massive datasets, and make real-time decisions offers unparalleled advantages (Figure 11.1).

Figure 11.1 AI and space technology.

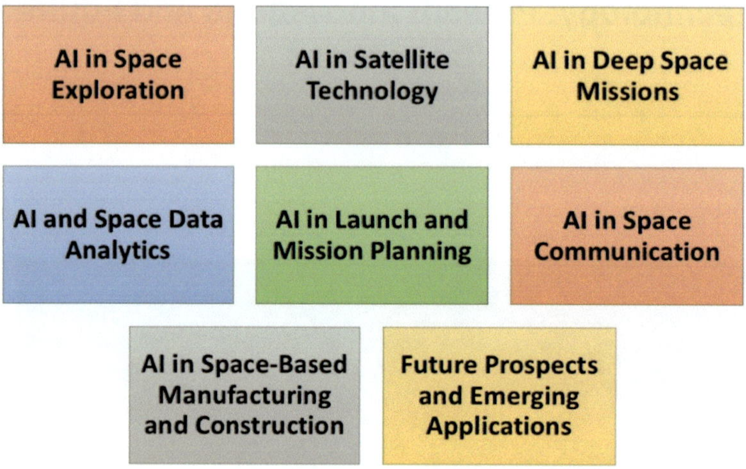

AI in Space Exploration

Mars Rovers and Autonomous Navigation

NASA's Perseverance Rover, which landed on Mars in 2021, is a prime example of AI's application in autonomous navigation. Equipped with an AI-powered system known as autonomous exploration for gathering increased science (AEGIS), Perseverance can make independent decisions about which rocks to examine and photograph, significantly enhancing its scientific productivity.

Similarly, the European Space Agency (ESA) and NASA have used AI for terrain recognition and obstacle avoidance, enabling rovers to travel greater distances with reduced input from Earth—a crucial feature given the communication delay of 5 to 20 minutes each way between Earth and Mars.

Robotic Assistants in Space Missions

NASA's Robonaut and the CIMON (crew interactive mobile companion) developed by Airbus for the International Space Station (ISS) are intelligent robotic assistants designed to support astronauts in complex environments. CIMON uses IBM Watson's AI to understand voice commands, recognize faces, and provide relevant information to astronauts, reducing cognitive load during missions.

AI in Satellite Technology

Earth Observation and Environmental Monitoring

Satellites equipped with AI capabilities are transforming environmental monitoring. For example, ESA's Copernicus program leverages AI algorithms to analyze satellite imagery for climate change indicators, deforestation, glacier movement, and natural disasters. These AI models can detect subtle changes in terrain, vegetation, and atmospheric conditions faster and more accurately than traditional methods.

Maxar Technologies, in collaboration with the U.S. government and humanitarian organizations, uses AI to process satellite data for real-time crisis response, including monitoring wildfires, floods, and conflict zones.

Satellite Health Monitoring

AI is also used to ensure the health and functionality of satellites. Machine learning algorithms analyze telemetry data to detect anomalies and predict potential failures. This predictive maintenance extends satellite lifespans and minimizes mission disruptions.

For instance, the Defense Advanced Research Projects Agency (DARPA) uses AI-driven diagnostics in its satellite constellations to enable on-the-fly problem detection and resolution without waiting for Earth-based human intervention.

AI in Deep Space Missions

Intelligent Spacecraft Control

AI is crucial in missions where real-time human intervention is impossible due to vast distances. The Deep Space Network (DSN), operated by NASA, uses machine learning to schedule communication sessions with distant spacecraft efficiently, optimizing bandwidth and reducing latency.

NASA's planned Europa Clipper mission will utilize onboard AI to autonomously decide when to record data or activate sensors during its flybys of Jupiter's moon Europa, where conditions are too extreme and time-sensitive for Earth-based decision-making.

Self-healing Systems

Future interplanetary missions demand spacecraft capable of autonomous self-diagnosis and repair. AI systems are being trained to detect faults in real time and reconfigure systems to maintain mission continuity. This approach mimics biological systems' resilience and will be vital for long-duration missions to Mars or deep space.

AI and Space Data Analytics

Astronomical Data Analysis

Astronomy generates vast amounts of data—from radio signals to optical imagery—and AI is helping astronomers sift through this data efficiently. The Vera C. Rubin Observatory in Chile, set to become operational in the mid-2020s, will collect over 20 terabytes of data every night. AI-driven tools will be essential for detecting transient astronomical events like supernovae, asteroids, or gravitational waves.

Google's DeepMind and NASA have collaborated on AI models that detect exoplanets in Kepler Space Telescope data, finding planets missed by earlier analysis due to signal noise or faint signatures.

Cosmic Object Detection and Classification

AI models trained on astronomical datasets are improving our ability to classify galaxies, predict asteroid trajectories, and identify potentially hazardous near-Earth objects (NEOs). Tools like Asteroid Data Hunter, developed by NASA, and Planetary Resources, use machine learning to scan telescope images for asteroids with higher precision than manual analysis.

AI in Launch and Mission Planning

Rocket Design and Simulation

SpaceX, Blue Origin, and other private space firms use AI to optimize rocket design and simulate launch scenarios. AI-driven simulations reduce the time and cost of development by predicting outcomes of millions of design variables—such as structural integrity, fuel dynamics, and aerodynamic behavior—before physical testing.

Launch Optimization

AI algorithms are increasingly used for mission planning and launch scheduling. For instance, AI can determine the optimal launch window, minimize fuel use, and calculate real-time trajectory adjustments. NASA's Artemis program incorporates such tools to plan crewed lunar missions efficiently.

AI-powered weather prediction models also help in determining suitable launch conditions, reducing delays due to unpredictable weather patterns.

AI in Space Communication

Optimizing Communication Networks

With hundreds of satellites forming constellations like Starlink and OneWeb, managing communication networks in space has become a complex task. AI helps to route data optimally, reduce signal interference, and manage bandwidth allocation. These intelligent networks are critical for expanding global internet access and enabling remote sensing applications.

Interplanetary Communication

AI is being developed to manage communication for interplanetary missions, including real-time language translation and contextual compression of messages. As missions travel further from Earth, efficient and intelligent data exchange becomes a necessity rather than a luxury.

AI in Space-based Manufacturing and Construction

In-situ Resource Utilization (ISRU)

Future space missions, especially to the Moon and Mars, aim to use local resources to produce water, oxygen, and construction materials. AI algorithms are being developed to monitor ISRU systems, control robotic arms, and optimize extraction processes in unfamiliar and variable extraterrestrial environments.

NASA's AI4Mars project explores how rovers and robotic systems can use AI to navigate terrain, identify usable resources, and operate autonomously on planetary surfaces.

3D Printing and Construction in Space

AI-guided 3D printing robots are planned to build habitats and infrastructure using lunar or Martian regolith. Companies like ICON and Contour Crafting are experimenting with AI-based construction systems for off-Earth living, essential for long-term colonization.

Future Prospects and Emerging Applications

AI and Space Tourism

As commercial space travel becomes viable, AI will be critical in ensuring passenger safety, managing life support systems, and personalizing onboard experiences. Autonomous piloting, medical monitoring, and AI-powered navigation will redefine how civilians experience space.

AI and the Search for Extraterrestrial Life

AI plays a crucial role in the search for extraterrestrial intelligence (SETI). By analyzing radio signals and other cosmic data, AI models can detect anomalies or patterns suggesting artificial sources. Breakthrough Listen, the largest SETI project to date, uses AI to scan petabytes of data for potential alien transmissions.

AI-driven Space Settlement

AI will be foundational for the creation of self-sustaining habitats on the Moon, Mars, and beyond. From regulating agriculture in controlled environments to managing social dynamics within isolated human colonies, AI's capabilities will be tested on a new frontier of autonomy and resilience.

Challenges and Ethical Considerations

Trust and Reliability

One major challenge is ensuring that AI systems are trustworthy and resilient under unknown or high-risk conditions. Space is an unforgiving environment, and errors can be catastrophic. Therefore, AI systems must be rigorously tested and include fail-safes.

Data Security

As space missions become more reliant on AI, cybersecurity becomes paramount. AI systems managing satellites, navigation, or communication can become targets for cyberattacks. Governments and companies must develop robust security protocols for AI-driven space assets.

Autonomy vs. Human Oversight

As AI becomes more capable, a philosophical and operational debate emerges: how much autonomy should AI have in space? The risk of AI making a critical decision without human input must be weighed against the impracticality of constant human oversight in deep-space conditions.

Toward an Intelligent Universe

Artificial intelligence is no longer an auxiliary tool in space technology—it is fast becoming its backbone. From planetary rovers and autonomous spacecraft to intelligent satellites and cosmic data analytics, AI is enhancing our ability to explore, understand, and inhabit the cosmos.

In the coming decades, as humanity sets its sights on permanent lunar bases, manned Mars missions, and interstellar exploration, AI will play a pivotal role. The dream of colonizing space is no longer confined to science fiction—it is a tangible objective, powered by the twin engines of AI and human ingenuity.

Space agencies, private space companies, and global research institutions must continue investing in AI research and governance to ensure these tools serve us safely and effectively. As we stand on the edge of a new space age, AI is not just accelerating the journey—it is redefining what is possible among the stars.

Index

For Product Safety Concerns and Information please contact our EU representative GPSR@taylorandfrancis.com Taylor & Francis Verlag GmbH, Kaufingerstraße 24, 80331 München, Germany